was to be Normal

For Sandy,
This book is my testi-
mony to glorify Jesus
Christ! It's all true.
Let it bless you.
Much Love,
Jo

all I ever wanted was to be Normal

From chains of addictions to the joys of freedom!

by Jo Twidwell

TATE PUBLISHING
AND ENTERPRISES, LLC

All scriptures are taken from the *New King James Version Bible* (NKJV).

According to the author, this entire book is a testimony, and all events truly happened as described. Several names, descriptions, entities, and incidents included in the story are based on the lives of real people.

The opinions expressed by the author are not necessarily those of Tate Publishing, LLC.

Published by Tate Publishing & Enterprises, LLC.
127 E. Trade Center Terrace | Mustang, Oklahoma 73064 USA
1.888.361.9473 | www.tatepublishing.com

Tate Publishing is committed to excellence in the publishing industry. The company reflects the philosophy established by the founders, based on Psalm 68:11,
"The Lord gave the word and great was the company of those who published it."

Cover design by Ivan Charlem Igot
Interior design by Angelo Moralde

Published in the United States of America

ISBN: 978-1-62854-572-2
1. Self-Help / Substance Abuse & Addictions / Alcohol
2. Religion / Inspirational
15.06.18

Acknowledgments

I want to thank Barbara Warren of Blue Mountain Editorial Service for editing this book and especially for her encouragement. (You can reach them at BarbaraWarrenBlueMountainEdit.com.)

Sunrise Ministries International is an outreach to bring restoration to those with addictions, compulsions, and childhood hurts. Sunrise seminars offer help, hope, and healing to all who want to break free from the roots of life's most persistent and controlling problems. If you are interested in starting a nondenominational support group through this ministry, contact Bob and JoAnn Atherton at sunriseint.org. In addition to the work in the USA since 1981, this ministry has equipped pastors and leaders in Russia, Ukraine, Estonia, Latvia, Israel, Africa, Canada, Singapore, Europe, and India.

Contents

Preface

What is normal?

Before I became a Christian, I paid $250 to have my natal chart read by a world-renowned astrologer. All that he told me seemed real and true, but it was not what I wanted to hear. That diabolical astrological reading led to a plan of suicide, which was diverted by events that are yet unknown but no longer mysterious.

I was 23 years young and had been living in Waikiki for two years, far from my hometown, Wichita, Kansas. I worked at a successful real estate company as co-founder and general manager, otherwise commonly known as a secretary who had enough gumption to convince a man, a stranger on the beach, that with his broker's license and his money, I could help him start a new company.

I was determined to begin a whole new life when I moved to Hawaii, but after two years, it seemed I still didn't fit in such a beautiful, peaceful place. I was play-acting with pretty faces and bronze-tanned bodies in elegant settings of fine crystal and chandeliers, or on large sailboats drifting lazily on the sparkling sea, or playing backgammon for high stakes on luxuriously smooth, sandy beaches. I had run away from the Midwestern doldrums and entered the race for money, success and the greatest need of all: freedom! I didn't know in those days my captor was the devil. I knew nothing of spiritual bondages.

When I left Wichita, I thought I could escape the humiliating reputation I had earned as an "easy lay." But the need for approval and attention from men had come with me across the ocean.

It was the early 1970s. The era of free love and women's liberation was in full swing. Gone were the days of a kiss at the lady's front door at the end of a date and the question, "May I see you again?" The only question was, "Your place or mine?" If the date was extended to the bedroom, the unspoken answer was, "Yes, I'd like to see you again." If not, it was a rejection, and the relationship went no further. T-shirts read, "So many men, so little time" and "If it feels good, do it." It always felt good, but it never felt right. My new life in paradise was no better than the dusty plains of Kansas, but at least the sun shone all year, and the real estate company had made the top-ten list in less than two years.

I was hoping to find real love and a universal understanding of life, and I thought the astrologer could give me some helpful direction. He was entertainingly mystical, complimentary and clever. He pumped me full of enough common-sense observations to move me to the edge of my chair, and I listened attentively to every word he spoke.

"This is a very exciting chart!" he concluded. "You love people and you really love to let your hair down and have fun! You're the life of every party! You should not even think about settling down, getting married and having two-point-five children. You will never have a white picket fence and youngsters playing in the yard. You're just not meant to be married."

Noticing my expression of doubt and disappointment, he continued, "I suppose you could be married, but it would have to be a long-distance, weekend relationship, so you could have fun with other men."

Defensively, I interjected, "I am a loyal person! I would never cheat on my husband!" (Never mind that I had been having affairs with married men since I was 18. It was they who had been unfaithful to their wives, I thought. I was sure that once I found the right man, I would be a supportive, loving, faithful wife, like my mother.)

"Yes, loyalty is one of your strengths," he replied, "but that's why you would be miserable if you got married. You would feel guilty when prompted with sexual urges that come so naturally for you. There's nothing wrong with being single. Married men could not survive without women like you. You should learn to accept your purpose in life and be exceedingly glad about it. There's no housework or diapers in your chart."

The astrologer had confirmed what I already knew. I was nothing more than a whore.

The appointment with the astrologer had taken my lunch hour, which had always included at least two alcoholic drinks. Having heard the devastating confirmation of my "purpose in life," the physical need for a drink was more than having missed the lunchtime pick-me-up. I didn't go back to work but to an open bar on the beach. I drank and cried and planned a way to end my life. The guilt, shame, anguish and loneliness I felt were more than enough fuel for determination to drive my car off the edge of a cliff. It would appear as a tragic accident of a drunk driver. I remember getting into my car and driving toward the cliff … but the next thing I remembered was waking up in my bed the next morning.

Losing time, perhaps several hours, and having no recollection of my activities during that time is explainable. I'd had a blackout. Several years later, I learned that a blackout is a symptom of alcoholism. It is a period of time in which one functions (consciously talking, walking, even driving) but doesn't remember any of it.

I was flabbergasted when I woke that morning, wondering why, in my drunken stupor and extreme depression, I didn't drive my car off the cliff? Who had steered me home and tucked me in bed? Some would say it was my own will to survive, to change my destiny. Yet, too many factual miracles have happened since 1972 to overlook the mighty hand of God protecting one who would later be called into His kingdom. Perhaps it was a guardian angel doing God's bidding. At that time, though, it was an unexplainable, mysterious, last chance to live a decent life, and I became obsessed with a quest to be normal.

Throughout the next year, I went from man to man looking for someone to fall in love with me. The first thing I was going to do when I got married was to build a white picket fence around my front yard so everyone who passed by would see it and know that the woman living there was normal. However, unable to avoid the lure of lust, I realized I was getting nowhere, hopping from bed to bed. To say I had a low self-esteem is an understatement. I thought I was unlovable, unless I undressed.

A year later, my dad died, the result of colon cancer. It was time to go home. I was 25 years old and still single. I longed to find a good man with good, wholesome, Midwestern values, like my dad. With him gone, I wondered if there was another honest man like him on earth. Even if there was, I knew I wasn't worthy of a good man, and I would never have a white picket fence. I was depressed and further away from my ideal of being normal than ever before.

When I was 26 years old, miserably stuck in Wichita, Kansas, I woke in a bed one morning lying next to a man I had never seen before. I'd had another blackout, but I still didn't know what was happening to my memory. I had remembered being at a lounge, sitting at the bar, playing a dice game with several men, but that man sleeping next to me was not one of them. I considered myself to be fortunate because, whoever this man was who had picked me up and taken me to his bed, at least he was not a rapist who might have dumped me on the side of a road or murdered me. I was thankful for that, but I felt deeply ashamed and afraid that I might not be as lucky the next time. That scare led me to a psychologist.

I told the doctor about my memory losses and shamefully admitted I had a problem with sex. He was interested in the latter and wanted to hear every detail of my sexual activities. After a battery of tests, he diagnosed me as being psychotic and said I would need several years of therapy with him. I knew I was sad, lonely, confused, abnormal and bad, but I couldn't believe I was psychotic. During the first few sessions, the doctor's body language was subtle and distant but suspiciously familiar, and I was on guard. When his sexual advance was undeniable, I ran out of his office. *If I can't trust my confession to a doctor,* I thought, *there is no one in the world I can trust.* I rushed to a bar and sat alone in a dark corner for hours, drinking and crying. I did a lot of that in those days.

At age 32, I learned about the Father, the Son and the Holy Ghost, and I was ecstatic! For the first time in my life, I could define the meaning, worth, purpose and destiny of my life. And all of it was good! Even though I knew I was not good, I believed God loved me anyway, and He could make me good. I attended church services Sunday mornings, Sunday evenings and Wednesday evenings, read my

Bible every day, quoted scriptures in conversations, blurting "Hallelujah" or "Glory to God" or "Praise the Lord." I was happy, but I was also aware that many people thought my behavior was not normal.

It didn't take long (just 15 days, described in Chapters 1 through 5) to realize that "normal according to Jesus" and "normal according to the world" are two different things.

One reason Jesus was born and lived in the form of man was to tell people how to live in the Kingdom of God right here on Earth. Many people believe in the heavenly Father, Jesus and the Holy Ghost. They go to church every Sunday religiously. Some even read the Bible. But I don't think most people, even Christians, would consider Jesus' way of living as normal. Yet, Jesus told us in the Bible to cast out demons, to pray for our enemies and forgive them, to lay hands on sick people for healing. Jesus made the lame to walk and the blind to see, and He raised the dead back to life! Jesus said,

"Most assuredly, I say to you, he who believes in Me, the works that I do he will do also; and greater works than these he will do." (John 14:12 NKJV)

I have done some of those things. God gave me the most precious of gifts—faith in Jesus—and through my faith, His power has been evident in my life. I believed what I read in the Bible, and miracles happened. That's "normal" in the Kingdom of God. That's the way God intended life for all of mankind to be.

Miracles are fascinating but not mysterious. I believe a miracle is an act of God, something no human being could do. But I don't think God considers them miracles, as we do. While miracles by human standards seem amazing and extraordinary, they are simple for God to do. A miracle is God's response to a person's faith, if it is according to God's Word (the Bible).

This book is a chronological collection of true, miraculous events that have happened in my life. So many miracles are described in the Bible, and so many miracles are happening all around us every day. God has not changed since Bible days. People change. Thank God, people can change the instant they begin to believe.

Faith in itself is a miracle. It is a gift from God available to all who desire it. But once given, it is our choice whether we use it or not.

Chapter 1

God answered my cry for help

I was living with my boyfriend, Robert, in Wichita, Kansas. We were planning to be married someday. I can't say that I loved him, but I knew all other options were gone. I was 32 years old and still single.

Robert was the only man I had ever known who could control me. I needed someone to love me and take care of me, so I let him control me. He set the rules, and I followed them. He yelled at me. He pushed and yanked and shook me. He hit my face. He forced his body upon mine, whether I wanted it or not.

He didn't have a job, but he had a wild imagination, which I translated into "ambition." He told me fantastically fabricated stories about his past and our future, and I chose to believe him.

When I met Robert, I had been working as a freelance copywriter, producing corporate newsletters, brochures and other types of literature for small companies, and I had recently lost four major accounts. I was barely getting by financially. There is no doubt I had lost those clients because of my constant drinking and depressed, apathetic moods.

When Robert told me he had a lot of money in a bank in Switzerland and we could get our hands on it soon, I quit working for the few clients I had left. When I told Robert what I had done, he got very mad and very drunk. He put a long, sharp butcher knife next to my throat and threatened to kill me if I ever did anything again without his permission. Out of fear, I said, "I'm sorry." Out of emptiness, I let him continue filling my head and my heart with lies.

My mother and my older sister, Bobbie, didn't like Robert. I defended him against all of their accusations. I told them, if they didn't accept Robert into our family, they would lose me. Unaware of my mental, emotional and spiritual illness, I was defensive, rebellious and blind. My illness was a strong opponent, even against the love of my family—but not against their prayers.

My mother arranged and paid for a cruise vacation, just for the three of us, secretly hoping she and Bobbie could talk some sense into me before I married Robert. On the day that Bobbie and I were to meet at Mother's house to drive together to the airport, Robert decided he would not let me go. He would not let me call Mother on the phone. He would not let me move from a seated position on the couch. He sat in front of me on the ottoman with a bottle of scotch in one hand and the other fist clenched, ready to attack if I would even move an arm or open my mouth to speak. I watched the hours go by on the wall clock. I was afraid of him, because I knew his behavior was insane, but I was growing angrier as the time to be at Mother's house approached. I hadn't even packed my bags for the cruise.

Finally, I was furious. I leaped from the couch and pushed him to the floor. I ran to the kitchen and took the long, sharp butcher knife from the drawer. Revenge boiled inside of me, and I wanted to kill him. He knew I was seriously threatening his life with the knife, so he let me push him and hit him with my other hand. I had never before been aware of nor expressed the emotion of anger, but many years of anger at myself came forth. I took a heavy mirror from the bedroom wall and threw it at his head. Glass shattered. Robert's arm was bleeding. He fell upon the bed and passed out.

I called my mother and she came to get me. It was a horrifying scene for her to see. I felt so ashamed.

Throughout the week ahead on the ship, I was severely depressed. I drank all day, every day and walked up and down the decks alone, sobbing, not caring who saw me crying. It was an expensive trip wasted and, I was convinced, mine was a wasted life.

When I returned to Robert, he was sweet, kind and charming, promising all of his love and good behavior and a wonderful life for the two of us. I knew it could never be. I knew there was no hope for me and no reason to live anymore.

I pretended to believe his promises, and we drank scotch to celebrate, straight from the bottle. He gulped long slugs while I sipped, waiting for him to pass out so I could finally put an end to my miserable life. This time, I would really do it.

When I was sure he was unconscious on the bed, I went to the living room and paced back and forth, trying to think of a sure way to kill myself. Occasionally, thoughts interrupted my planning. Thoughts of my mother, my older sister Bobbie, my younger sister Debbie, and a few friends, which made me cry. But, even then, I thought they would be much better off, not having to constantly worry about what trouble I would conjure up next. The only thought that caused a sharp pain in my heart was that they would be sad for a while, especially at my funeral. After all, they had told me they loved me. They were always there to clean-up the messes I had made.

My heart was heavy. I dropped to the floor on bended knees, and my head rested on folded arms on the cold, seat-ledge of the fireplace. I tried to think of reasons not to kill myself. I tried to find some hope, some dream that I could make myself believe would come true, but nothing came to mind. Nothing good. I decided there was nothing good in the world.

Exhausted, I lifted my head, faintly determined to proceed and be done with it. The brick fireplace in front of me and the gray ashes reminded me of an altar. What made me think of that, I don't know. But the altar image made me think of God. I wondered if there really was such a thing as God.

A tickling sensation in my stomach made me think I was hungry, but the feeling moved upward, and I actually felt my heart flutter. It moved higher and my throat clogged. I could not swallow or speak or breathe. As quickly as panic took hold of me, the lump in my throat thrust upward and burst into a million particles, tingling my spine and tickling my scalp. I was light-headed, giddy and glad.

It had been many years since I had felt that sort of sensation. It reminded me of fireworks igniting in me, exploding into brilliant colors the instant I had met Larry, my first love, 12 years earlier. The feeling that flowed through me was hope.

It was just a glimmer of hope, but it was as real as the ache still lodged in my heart. The room was dark and the spark of hope was gone as suddenly as it came, like a falling star that landed somewhere far away.

I rolled over, lying flat on the floor on my stomach. My forehead pressed heavily on the backs of my hands. I took a deep breath and thought about that feeling … that gush of hope. It had happened when I was pondering the possibility that there might really be a God somewhere in a place called heaven.

My eyelids scrunched tightly together, guarding myself from being fooled again by the desperate need of love. My fists clenched in fighting mode, but the need was still there.

Hope? Despair! Maybe? No! Possible? Not possible! Future? Fantasy! My thoughts and emotions were vacillating up and down, with energy mounting then plunging and crashing at the bottom of a pit. Every muscle in my body was clenched, and I wanted the tornadic whirl of confusion to *stop!*

I sat up, looked up and cried out like a child whimpering helplessly, "If there is a God … if you can hear me … help me! Please, help me!"

I sobbed the most agonizing, hopeless fit of crying that I had ever allowed myself to release. In the midst of my wailing, I heard a voice.

"There is a church across the street. Go there tomorrow."

I gasped when I heard it and held my breath. Quickly, I looked around the room to see who was there. No one. I turned on all of the lights, and then I went to the bedroom and found Robert still unconscious. I poked him, but he didn't move. I slapped his face, but his eyelids didn't flinch.

I went to the window in the living room and peeked through the drapes to see what was across the street, but the blackness of night was thick, and I could see nothing.

I repeated the words in my mind over and over again. *There is a church across the street. Go there tomorrow.*

"There's no church across the street!" I blurted out loud.

I had lived with Robert in that duplex for three months. I had driven down that street so many times. I had never seen a church anywhere on that street. Of that, I was certain. But I was also certain I had heard those words. Not inside my head but outside of my ears, as if a man, standing closely behind me, had softly spoken those words. "There is a church across the street. Go there tomorrow."

Dubious and exhausted, I fell asleep on the couch.

The next morning, as soon as I awoke, I ran to the window and looked across the street. There was no church there. Only the back side of a small strip shopping center. I knew that building was there. I had driven by it daily, but I could not think of what shops were in the building. I was curious and suspicious of the words I had heard the night before.

Robert was asleep. Quickly, I pulled on a jacket and tennis shoes and quietly opened the front door. I tiptoed across the street, as a burglar would approach a dark house, stalking it. There were several doors along the back of the building. Slowly and carefully, afraid I would be caught snooping by a shop owner, I opened the nearest door.

It was a huge room. Many rows of chairs on golden carpet. An oak podium stood tall on a stage, and on the wall, behind the podium, was a large wooden cross. Above the cross were the words, "JESUS CHRIST IS LORD."

It is a church! I could hardly believe my eyes.

Chapter 2

I saw God's light

I stepped into the sanctuary, just as Dorothy had stepped out of her wind-torn house with wonder in her eyes when she saw the vivid colors of Munchkin land. Amazed but cautious.

It being a weekday, I wondered why so many people were there. Children were mingling around chairs, and a few adults were on the stage. There was an echoing buzz, everyone talking within their small groups of friends. No one noticed me. Slowly, I walked across the rear of the massive room to the wall. I walked up the wall aisle toward the front, passing a few rows, and sat on a cold, gray, folding chair. It seemed I was invisible, yet I could see people moving and talking and laughing. I slid down low in the chair, rested the back of my neck on the top of the chair and closed my eyes.

This is too hard to believe, I thought. *But I did hear that voice last night, and this is a church. Could that have been the voice of God?*

I opened my eyes and bright lights on the ceiling caused me to squint. I rubbed my eyes and looked up again. There on the ceiling was the shape of a large cross made of rectangular fluorescent lights, six vertical and four across.

My eyes were sore and swollen. Both hands covered my face and I lowered my head to rest on my knees so I would not be seen. I felt dirty and ugly. I had rushed out of the house without combing my hair. I hadn't washed my face or brushed my teeth. My clothes were shaggy and soiled. But I was barely aware of my outward appearance. Inside, I quivered, feeling filthy and grimy—too hideous to be in such a clean, sterile place. I tried to quiet my crying, holding my mouth.

I felt a hand on my shoulder. A large woman stood beside me in the aisle. Without a word, she shoved me gently, and I moved to the next chair. As she sat down, her heavy arm laid across my shoulders.

She sat silently while I wiped the tears and rubbed my eyes. Then, my vision focused on her face. It was a beautiful face with big, dark-brown, sparkling eyes. The wrinkles framing her eyes deepened as she smiled, and she spoke with a gentle, pleasing voice and with absolute assurance. "It's going to be all right now. You've come to the right place."

That's all she said. She wrapped her big arms around me and squeezed my body, a bear hug the likes of which I'd never felt before. And she didn't let go. She held me as

I cried, my head buried in her wide, soft shoulder. We sat there together for what seemed a long time in each other's arms. She knew I couldn't talk just yet.

When finally I could breathe without gasping, I cleared my throat and straightened myself in the chair. I couldn't look at her eyes, but I was comforted knowing they were looking at me, patient and kind.

"I'm a mess," I said, feeling embarrassed about my sloppy appearance. "My whole life is a mess."

"Would you like to talk to someone? A counselor?"

I took a deep breath. "I don't know. I don't know what to do."

"Wait here," she said, as she took my hands in hers. "I'll be right back." She squeezed my hands gently and then walked away.

Moments later I was sitting in a small office. A short man walked in and sat at the desk.

"My name is Rick," he said. He turned his attention to papers on the desk, gathering them and placing them in neat piles.

I felt a sense of panic mounting within me. I didn't want to be there. I felt nauseous, and I couldn't get comfortable in that chair. My hands clasped together, palms rubbing each other back and forth. I wanted to run away.

He began talking, but I didn't look at him and I didn't hear what he was saying. I looked all around the small room. The word "Jesus" was everywhere—on a poster, on a painting, on a paperweight. Then I noticed he wasn't talking. His hands were folded together on the desk. He was looking at me, waiting for me to speak.

"This was probably a mistake for me to come here," I said meekly.

"I don't think it was a mistake at all," he said. His voice was soft and low and friendly. "There must be a reason you're here."

Should I tell him? I wondered. *Should I tell him that God spoke to me last night and told me to come here? He'll think I'm crazy!*

"Is there something you want to talk about?" he asked.

I didn't know where to begin. There was too much to tell, and I knew he wouldn't understand. He sat there, waiting. Suddenly, I blurted, "It's nothing in particular. It's everything. It's life in general." My voice grew louder with each statement. "I just can't live anymore!"

My chin crumpled and my lips pressed tightly together. I held my breath. I tried to hold my body still, but it quivered.

Rick got up and walked around the desk toward me. He knelt beside my chair and held my hands. I watched his face as he closed his eyes and prayed.

I don't remember what he said in that prayer, but I do remember feeling settled, calmed, even comfortable in that big, cushioned chair. He gave me a cup of cold water, and it felt good on my dry tongue.

Rick returned to his desk, and I began telling him how terrible my life was. I told him about Robert, that we were living together and we were supposedly going to be married. Neither of us had a job. We had a lot of bills but no money. I told him I was tired. I just couldn't make anything work, and I didn't want to try anymore.

Rick leaned forward on the desk. He looked straight into my eyes and said, "Do you realize you are living in sin?"

Sin? My first impulse was to defend myself against such a slanderous remark. I didn't know exactly what he meant by that, but I was sure it was rude and insulting. I opened my mouth to object, but I was mute.

The only way I know how to describe the next few seconds or minutes is to say I was in another place. I don't know where I was, but Rick wasn't there. The desk wasn't there. I couldn't see anything but light. The light was all around me. I felt that flicker of hope well up inside of me, and it filled me completely. It seemed I was weightless, as if I was floating. No one spoke to me, yet I knew what was being said. God was telling me that He loved me very much. It didn't matter what I had done. He loved me anyway. He loved me when I was good, and He loved me when I was bad. He had loved me all of my life. He told me it was true, that I had been living in sin, and the sin was hurting me. He was sad about that. It made Him sad to watch me, because he loved me so much, and He didn't want me to be hurt. He said He could make all the sins be gone. Nothing was so bad that He couldn't take care of it. It would be simple for Him, and He would gladly do it for me.

I felt lovely and soft and white, like a fluffy, drifting cloud, and I knew that everything would be all right now. Everything would be all right.

I was slightly dazed when Rick came into focus. He didn't seem to notice that I had been somewhere else. He asked if I wanted to pray with him, to let go of the past and let Jesus take care of me.

My skin tingled from my toes to the top of my head. I had never seen the truth so clearly as in that moment. I answered, "Yes, I have been living in sin. I didn't realize it until now. I don't want to live that way anymore! I want to talk to God. I want to tell him I'm sorry. Can we pray right now?"

Rick led me through a prayer of repentance and salvation. He said, "Repeat what I say out loud, if you really mean it in your heart."

When he said, "Lord, forgive me for all of my sins," I said, "Lord, forgive me for all of my sins. I am so sorry for everything I've done to make you sad. I didn't know you were watching me. I didn't even know you were real! I don't want to do any more sins, God. I want to do good things. If you will make all of those bad sins go away from me, then everything will be all right, and we can be happy and laugh, and we won't be sad anymore. I promise."

Then Rick said, "Come into my life, Jesus, and be my Lord and Savior," I said, "Thank you, Jesus, for coming into my life today. I want you to be my Lord and Savior every day from now on."

When the prayer was finished, Rick was in awe of my open, eager response but exclaimed that he was pleased and thankful. He said I should buy a Bible and start reading the book of John and that I should come to the worship service on Sunday morning at ten o'clock. Rick marked appointments on his desk calendar for me to come to his office for a counseling session the next day, then once each week thereafter. He gave me a booklet of Bible lessons, and I was to have a lesson done before each weekly appointment. I could hardly wait to get started.

Chapter 3

There really is power in the name of Jesus

Before I left Rick's office on the day I was saved, he asked, "What do you plan to do about Robert?"

"I'm going to tell him everything that has happened to me today, and I'm going to bring him in to see you. I'm sure he doesn't know God really exists. We've got to help him, too!"

"Yes, we'll help Robert, too," he said lovingly, "but, in the meantime, will you continue living with him?"

"Oh. Living with him is a sin, isn't it?"

Rick grinned and nodded his head up and down.

"But where will I live? I don't have any money. What will Robert think of that? I don't think Robert is going to like this idea at all!"

Suddenly, I felt the familiar grip of fear, like two heavy hands strangling my throat. I had not told Rick that Robert was physically abusive, not to mention insane.

"Do you have relatives in town?" Rick asked.

"Yes, my mother and a sister. I could live with my mother for a while. But maybe I should wait until Robert has a chance to come here and understand why we shouldn't be living together. I'm afraid he's going to be awfully upset."

"Are you afraid of Robert?"

"Sometimes I am."

"God will be with you wherever you are. You have nothing to fear. Do you know why?"

I tilted my head inquisitively.

"Because there is power in the name of Jesus," he said. "Remember that!"

Rick talked about Jesus briefly. What stuck in my mind was that I had authority over the devil, because Jesus had already fought with the devil long ago, and Jesus had won.

"Since you belong to Jesus now," Rick explained, "the devil can't hurt you anymore. Don't be afraid. I think you should move to your mother's house today. Ask God to help you, and ask it in the name of Jesus."

I left the church through the front door. Standing in the parking lot, I looked at the front of the long, brick building. The name of the church, Wichita Christian Center, was attached to the front of the building on the end furthest away from the duplex, where I lived with Robert. There were no signs in the parking lot or by the street. No wonder I hadn't known it was a church.

Light-hearted, yet slightly apprehensive, I briskly walked across the street, talking to God out-loud.

"Okay, God, here goes. I'm going to tell Robert that you're real, and I'm going to tell him we should not be living together, and I'm going to pack my things and go to Mother's house. He might be awfully mad, you know. It's a good thing you're going with me. Help me explain to him that everything will be all right. In the name of Jesus."

When I entered the house, Robert wasn't there. *He probably went out for cigarettes,* I thought. I packed a small bag of necessities and sat on the couch, waiting for him to come home. I wanted to tell him about the church across the street and the fluorescent cross on the ceiling and the beautiful woman who was so kind to me and the light. I was sure, if he could be in that light and know how wonderful and loving God is, he would understand.

I waited, but he didn't come home. I wrote a note, telling Robert I'd had a fantastic experience and had learned some important things, and I would tell him all about it. I wrote that I was moving to Mother's house, and I would call to explain everything.

That evening on the phone, Robert listened while I talked non-stop. He agreed, it had been a remarkable day for me, but he said he was lonely and needed me and couldn't live without me. He wanted me to come back, and he promised we would go to that church together, as a couple, every Sunday morning. He seemed sad, and I felt sorry for him but excited for him at the same time, knowing he would understand as soon as he talked to God.

I assured him, "I will make an appointment for you to see Rick when I'm there tomorrow. My appointment is at three o'clock, and then I'll stop by the house to see you."

When I entered the church the next day, children were scurrying everywhere. While waiting for Rick, the receptionist told me about the Christian academy, kindergarten through high school. She gave me a schedule listing the meeting times of the singles' group, the ladies' Bible study group, the home fellowships, the monthly pot-luck dinner and the evening Christian college classes. "We're just one big family," Pam said.

A person's entire social life could be within the walls of this building, I thought. I hadn't had a social life for several years. I felt safe there, and I was anxious to get involved with all of it, especially if the people were as nice and friendly as Pam and Rick and the woman with the brown eyes.

Rick greeted me, and we went to his office. I showed him the Bible, which I had purchased with the money my mother had given to me. Rick told me to find Luke, the third book in the New Testament, chapter eight, and he asked me to read out loud verses 4 through 15.

4 "And when a great multitude had gathered, and they had come to Him from every city, He spoke by a parable:

5 "A sower went out to sow his seed. And as he sowed, some fell by the wayside; and it was trampled down, and the birds of the air devoured it.

6 "Some fell on rock; and as soon as it sprang up, it withered away because it lacked moisture.

7 "And some fell among thorns, and the thorns sprang up with it and choked it.

8 "But others fell on good ground, sprang up, and yielded a crop a hundredfold." When He had said these things He cried, "He who has ears to hear, let him hear!"

9 Then His disciples asked Him, saying, "What does this parable mean?"

10 And He said, "To you it has been given to know the mysteries of the kingdom of God, but to the rest it is given in parables, that 'Seeing they may not see, And hearing they may not understand.'

11 "Now the parable is this: The seed is the word of God.

12 "Those by the wayside are the ones who hear; then the devil comes and takes away the word out of their hearts, lest they should believe and be saved.

13 "But the ones on the rock are those who, when they hear, receive the word with joy; and these have no root, who believe for a while and in time of temptation fall away.

14 "Now the ones that fell among thorns are those who, when they have heard, go out and are choked with cares, riches, and pleasures of life, and bring no fruit to maturity.

15 "But the ones that fell on the good ground are those who, having heard the word with a noble and good heart, keep it and bear fruit with patience." (Luke 8:4-15)

When I lifted my head, Rick asked, "Which do you think you will be?"

I reviewed Jesus' explanation of the parable, following my finger on the page of the book, as Rick continued.

"Will you let the devil take the Word of God out of your heart?"

"No," I replied.

"Will you believe for a little while and then, when you're tempted, fall away?"

"No, I hope not. And I couldn't possibly be choked with the cares and riches and pleasures of this life. I lived the so-called 'good life' in Hawaii for four years. Believe me, it wasn't good for me."

"Well then, do you think the Word of God will be planted like a seed on good ground, in your heart?"

Rick waited. Silently, I read verse 10 again.

10 "To you it has been given to know the mysteries of the kingdom of God."

All of my life had been a mystery. I was fed up with wandering and searching without a clue, and I wanted to know the truth. I was sick and tired of the constant ache in my heart, year after year, with no relief. The ache had gone away the day before (when I was in the light and God told me He loved me), and I hadn't felt the heartache since then.

I looked at Rick and boldly replied, "I think God thinks I have a good heart."

Rick smiled. "I think you have a good heart, too."

He closed his book and glanced at his watch. He leaned back comfortably in his chair and looked at me as if we were finished, but the hour wasn't up yet. I didn't want to go. I wanted to read more, but Rick wanted to talk about Robert.

"He's sad about my moving out," I reported. "You must make an appointment right away for him to talk to you."

Rick agreed and penciled Robert's name on the next day of his calendar. "Meanwhile, when you're with him, someone else ought to be with you, too."

"What do you mean?"

"I mean, you should not be alone with him."

"That's ridiculous," I chuckled. "We're going to be married."

"But you're not married yet. You ought to let him court you ..."

"With a chaperone?" I interrupted. "Are you serious?"

"Yes, I am serious. You and Robert are accustomed to a certain lifestyle. You are familiar with each other, and it may not be easy for Robert to resist temptations. Do you know what I mean?"

"Yes, I see. You're right about that."

"And, I don't want you to be tempted either. Those whose seed fell upon a rock heard the Word of God, and they received it with joy, but they had no root. When temptation came, they fell away."

"I don't want that to happen," I said absolutely.

"It will take some time for you and Robert to develop roots, as you learn more about God."

There wasn't anything in the world I wanted more than to learn more about God. I told Rick I understood what he was saying, and I sincerely thanked him for all of his help.

As I was leaving Rick's office, I saw the large woman with the beautiful, brown eyes talking to someone in the hallway. I approached them and stood there. When she noticed me, she stopped talking and smiled. Words were not necessary when our eyes met.

Her eyes said, *Thank God, you've come back!*

My eyes said, *Thank you!*

We talked briefly, and I learned her name, Jackie Gough. She gave me another bear hug and said she was very happy for me.

I went to my car in the parking lot feeling special. I felt good about having a good heart and excited about what I had learned in the Bible. There was a new seed planted somewhere inside my heart, and I was responsible for taking good care of it so it would grow.

As I drove through the parking lot, I remembered that I had told Robert I would stop by the house after my appointment with Rick. I thought about Rick's suggestion, that I should not be alone with Robert. But I promised myself, I would stay only a moment, just long enough to tell Robert the time of his appointment with Rick the next day.

When I stepped onto the front porch, I felt awkward ringing the doorbell of what had been my own house. Robert opened the door, grabbed my arm and yanked me inside. He pulled me close to his body. His lips pressed hard against mine. He was crushing me and smearing my face with his mouth. I tried to push myself away, but his grip was firm. Finally, he stopped, and his face was one inch away from my face.

His eyes were frightening. The whites of his eyes were not white at all and not bloodshot red as usual, but yellow. His pupils were piercing, and all around the black bullets was murky, mustard yellow.

He whirled me around with one strong hand, squeezing my arm, and he pulled me into the bedroom. He threw me upon the bed and glared at me with hateful yellow eyes. My arms were frozen. Air filled my lungs, but I could not let the air out.

He climbed on top of me, straddling my waist. With one hand, he grabbed the front of my blouse, ripped it, and spread it open.

"Robert, don't!" I shouted. But I knew he wouldn't stop.

I thought of my new friends and my new social life in the building across the street. It was so near, yet so far away. I thought about the promise I had made to God, that I would not make Him sad anymore.

Robert's hands were at my waist, unzipping my jeans. His yellow eyes and hot breath reminded me of the devil.

The devil must be in Robert, I thought. *But Rick promised the devil wouldn't hurt me anymore.*

He pulled my jeans down to my knees, scraping my thighs with his nails.

I thought about the seed that was planted in my heart. *I have to protect it! I can't give-up!*

I braced my hands on Robert's chest just before he lowered his body onto mine. His weight was heavy, and the pain in my wrists shot through my arms. I jerked my head left and right, escaping his darting mouth. One of his hands moved downward, between my legs. When he lifted his head to shift his weight, I looked at those yellow eyes and yelled, "In the name of Jesus! Get off of me!"

In a fraction of a second, I heard a thump on the wall. I lifted my head and saw Robert lying on the floor, unconscious, fourteen feet away from me on the other side of the room.

Cautiously, I sat up and stared at the still lump of Robert crumpled on the carpet. I scanned the distance between me and the wall, trying to comprehend the incredible magnitude of such a feat. *He must have flown across the room in a flash!*

Amazed but convinced, I whispered, "There really is power in the name of Jesus."

An exhilarating rush of excitement flowed through me as I thought about what Rick had said. *I do have authority over the devil! Because I belong to Jesus!*

A chuckle gushed out, and then another, and soon I was laughing. My head fell back on the bed, and I laid there laughing deliriously. All of the tension and fear was being laughed out, and I was sure I would never be afraid again. It was funny, imagining Robert flying across the room and crashing against the wall; but more than that, it was a great relief, a secure feeling of safety from any offender.

It had been so many years since I had laughed like that. I was laughing at the devil, and I was laughing at myself, happily grasping the simplicity of it all. And it seemed that Jesus was there in the room, laughing with me, too.

I checked to make sure Robert was breathing, and then I left. I didn't tell anyone about Jesus throwing Robert across the room. I didn't think my mother or sisters or friends would believe it. I didn't tell my new friends at the church, because they already knew about "the power in the name of Jesus." I assumed miracles like that happened to them all the time.

Chapter 4

Hand in hand

I felt like a spectator on that first Sunday morning. The praise and worship service was unlike anything I had ever seen before. They didn't sing from hymn books. There was an overhead projector at the front of the sanctuary, and they sang words that appeared on a large screen. At the bottom of most of the songs was the scripture reference.

The small orchestra was impressive. The drummer kept the beat and sometimes made the songs more dramatic, and the trumpet perked-up the rhythm to add a little jazziness. A violin, of course, pulled at the heart strings. There was a clarinet, a trombone, a flute, a piano, a guitar, and what looked like a big guitar that was as tall as the person playing it. Music was not my forte. Aside from not knowing the name of the big guitar, I was reluctant to sing out loud, knowing I would disturb the people standing on either side of me.

Everyone was standing throughout the entire worship service. Almost everyone in that huge room raised their hands when they sang. I thought that was more than a little strange, until I looked closer at the expressions on their faces. The worship leaders on the stage, two women and a man, each tilted their head upward and stretched their arms high in the air, as if they were reaching to catch something that would fall from above. But their eyes were closed. It appeared they were deeply concentrating their attention and affection upward. They were singing to God.

I watched the people standing close to me, and they were likewise positioned. The most amazing thing I noticed was that their faces seemed to glow.

The music was lovely, and the words they were singing were plain and simple. I realized they were love songs when these words came on the screen: "I love you, Lord, and I lift my hands, to worship you, oh my soul rejoice!"

The words, combined with the beautiful music and the loving expressions on the people's faces, made me realize this was not a performance. It was not like a choir providing their musical talent for the audience's enjoyment. It was a deep, personal expression of love for God. Everyone was doing it together, yet each individual seemed to be in their own world, singing from their own heart.

One woman looked so happy. Her eyes were closed, and she was smiling as she sang. Then, a single tear crept from the outer corner of one eye and flowed through the wrinkle at the edge of her smile.

She must be able to see something beautiful, I thought. *It must be something so wonderful and touching that it brought a tear to her eye.*

I closed my eyes but saw nothing. The music was all around me, but I felt alone in my own black space. I wondered what it was that she could see behind closed eyes. It was almost perplexing enough for me to ask her later, but she was one of many with that same look on her face, so I didn't ask.

It was probably one of those things, I thought, *that everyone in the world knows, except me.*

The worship service that evening was quite the same, but fewer people were there. Everyone's eyes were closed, their arms reaching upward. Even the little children's. If I thought those people were strange that morning, I felt even stranger that evening because I was the only person there whose eyes were not closed and whose arms were rigidly molded to my sides, singing a love song into the air.

The rhythm of the next song was livelier, and everyone clapped their hands with the beat of the music. Their eyes were open and all of the faces were smiling. I had never seen such a happy group of people in my whole life. When a person looked at me with a big smile on his or her face, it made me smile, too.

The lively song they were singing was about having victory in Jesus. It went like this: "I heard an old, old story, how a savior came from glory, how he gave his life on Calvary, and saved a wretch like me." We sang that song at least five times without stopping. I wondered why they didn't go on to another song, but I liked the beat of that song, so I clapped my hands and sang along with everyone else. I really got into that song and loosened up. I didn't know what some of the words meant, but I knew there was power and victory in the name of Jesus. I thought about Robert flying across the bedroom and crashing against the wall, and I knew Jesus had done that to rescue me.

"Oh, victory in Jesus ..." The more I sang it, the louder I sang, and I didn't care if I was off key.

"He saved a wretch like me ..." I knew I wasn't worth a second glance, yet Jesus had literally saved my life when He told me to come to this place.

"Then I repented of my sins and won the victory ..." *It's true,* I thought. *It happened just like that!* "Oh, victory in Jesus, my savior forever ..."

I looked up, and my eyes became fixed on the fluorescent cross on the ceiling. I stopped singing and whispered, "Thank you, Jesus. I don't know how to thank you, but I really mean it."

I stared at the lighted cross, thinking of the spectacular events since Wednesday of the past week. New experiences, new feelings, new knowledge and awareness. Only four days ago, I had thought there was no strength in me to try anymore, and I couldn't bear to think of struggling through the years of life ahead.

But now, I thought, *I am standing in a place that I didn't know existed. I am actually singing! I have a huge book that contains a wealth of knowledge that is written in such a clever way to reveal all the secrets of happiness, and I can hardly wait to read all of it!*

The depth and weight of gratitude grew in me. It was alive, moving and stirring within my heart. It wasn't play-acting. It wasn't being nice so I could get something nice in return. It was having so much without deserving it and without having to pay for it. I wanted to take the gratitude out of my heart and give it to Jesus for everything He had done for me. My arms slowly drifted up, stretching high in the air, not to catch but to give.

The music continued but gracefully moved into a new, slow melody. I closed my eyes and listened to the words: "As the deer panteth for the water, so my soul longeth after thee. You alone are my heart's desire and I long to worship thee. You alone are my strength, my shield. To you alone may my spirit yield. You alone are my heart's desire, and I long to worship thee."

I didn't sing. I listened to the words, standing in my own small space, snuggled in the comfort of the music, safely surrounded by good people who didn't care if I shut my eyes. I was alone, yet I was a part of the whole. It was dark and quiet in the privacy of my black space, but the music was all around me like a soft cushion. My arms were reaching toward heaven, like a child wanting to be lifted up. My eyes searched for something beautiful to see, while I talked to Jesus in my heart.

These people know so much more than I do, Jesus. They know you, and they love you, and they can probably even see you. It makes them happy to be so close to you. I want to know everything about you, too, Jesus. I wish I could know everything right now. But there is so much I don't understand.

Where are you, Jesus? Are you up there? Or right next to me? I know you are real, but I wish you could be real enough so I could be with you and hug you and hold your hand, and we could talk to each other. Oh, that's silly, isn't it?

It's so dark here. I wish I could see you as they do. If I could really see you and know you, then I would know everything, wouldn't I?

Oh, Jesus, I don't want to be alone anymore!

Yearning and searching alone in the darkness frightened me. I wanted to open my eyes, but my lashes were glued with thick, gooey tears. My fingers were entwined in prayer position, my hands squeezed together and pressed against my chest. My prayer echoed in the vast emptiness of my heart and my mind, silently shouting in earnest, *Jesus? Jesus! Where will I find you?*

The darkness became gray and transparent, like a light fog, and I thought I could see in the distance faint colors and vague shapes. It seemed to be moving toward me. Then, a picture came into focus. The colors were bright and rich and vividly sharp.

I saw a tree, a large tree with a mammoth trunk. I saw the profile of a young girl sitting on soft, green grass, leaning against the rough, brown bark of the tree. Her arms were wrapped around bent knees, and her head was bowed down, her face buried in the round circle of arms. There was lush green grass everywhere, as far as I could see, sparkling with dew and embracing tiny flowers. The flowers were dressed in pink, yellow, red and purple. The grass and the flowers were so bright and beautiful, but the girl seemed sad, sitting there alone. I could feel her loneliness, and I even understood that she didn't care about the beauty all around her.

Slowly, she lifted her head, and I saw her face. It was me! I was looking at myself in a picture, like an exquisite oil painting, but the picture was real and alive. I saw myself looking at a narrow, rocky path nestled in the grass directly in front of me, about three feet away. I watched myself sitting there, staring at the small rocks, feeling stuck to the ground and glued to the tree, lifeless and unable to move. Not even wanting to move. Just staring at the rocky path.

Then, I saw my head slowly turn away and tilt upward. I looked beyond where I was sitting in the picture. The rocky pathway led to the foot of a mountain. The path curved and made a trail all the way up the steep slope. At the top of the mountain, I saw a man. He was far away, but I could see his stature, and I knew that I—the small girl in the picture—could see the man, too, from down there on the ground. I could see the whole picture now: me by the tree and the backside of the man at the top of the mountain. He wore a long, red cape over his shoulders that draped down to his feet.

The man turned around and looked at me sitting on the ground. It was Jesus! I don't know how I knew it was Jesus, but I knew it absolutely. He lifted one hand, palm up, and He straightened His arm toward me, down below.

The colors faded, then the picture was gone, and all I could see was black space. I searched through the darkness, frantically trying to see the colors again, but everything was black. I tried to imagine the mountain. I tried to feel the loneliness I had felt when the picture had first appeared. I squeezed my eyelids tightly together, searching through black space. But I could see nothing. The picture was gone.

I opened my eyes, and everyone was still singing, "As the deer panteth for the water, so my soul longeth after thee."

I will never forget this song, I thought. *I'll never forget that instant when I looked up and saw Jesus at the top of that mountain!* Smiling, I wondered if everybody in the sanctuary had seen the same picture that I had seen.

Throughout the next three days, I thought about that picture a lot. Remembering how lonely I felt in that crowded room of happy strangers and how desperately I wanted to see Jesus, I reasoned that He had heard my plea and had granted me one quick glance. But He was so far away at the top of the mountain. As I thought more about it, I felt disconnected. I had been way down there on the ground, feeling sad and lonely, and Jesus was way up there at the top of the mountain. There was so much distance between us.

On Wednesday evening, I went to church and sang and raised my hands in the air. I smiled when people smiled at me, feeling relaxed and glad to be there again. I clapped my hands when the beat of the music was bouncy. I swayed back and forth with the slow songs and closed my eyes.

While everyone was singing, each in their own space, I retreated to mine. I longed to see Jesus again. I lifted my head and searched all around the blackness, looking for the top of the mountain, while I shared my thoughts with Jesus. I thanked Him for telling me to come to this place.

I like being here, I said in my heart, *and I like this music. Everyone has been so nice to me. And I am learning so many wonderful things about you in my Bible. I love my Bible.*

I opened my eyes and knelt to the floor to pick it up. I held my Bible close to my heart, crossing my hands over it, closed my eyes and continued my conversation.

If I hadn't read this book, I never would have known about you. I read that you are the good shepherd, and you take care of all of your sheep.

I thought about Jesus standing at the top of the mountain, as I had seen Him in the picture, and I whispered, "But why must you be so far away?"

Searching higher and higher in the darkness behind closed eyes, I desperately wanted to see Jesus in the picture again.

Suddenly, I saw it! The green grass and the flowers, the huge tree trunk and my small body propped against it. The whole scene was exactly as I had seen it on Sunday night, but Jesus was not at the top of the mountain. He was halfway up the steep slope, walking toward the top. The long, red cape draped down to his bare feet, treading on the rocky path. He turned around and looked at me, sitting on the ground. He extended one arm, with His palm up, and stretched it toward me again.

The colors turned black, and He was gone. After a few blinks and a deep breath, I joined in the singing, but my thoughts dwelled on the pictures.

Jesus had extended His hand toward me in both pictures, and I decided His gesture was an invitation for me to come to Him and take His hand and trek up the rugged mountain with Him. The mountain was surely a depiction of life, and the rocky path uphill indicated it would not be an easy jaunt. I would need His support and guidance. I would need to take hold of His hand. *I'll do it!* I promised. *Somehow, I will climb that mountain and take hold of your hand!* Determined and confident, I lifted my arms in the air and continued singing with a smile on my face and a heart full of hope.

Sunday morning could not have arrived soon enough. I went to church early and waited impatiently for the band to begin.

My conversations with Jesus by now were constant throughout the events of each day. I thanked Him for every good thing that happened. I asked Him specific questions about peculiar statements in the Bible or questions about people or places or the weather or what dress I ought to wear. He was my constant companion. But it was during the worship service in church that I thought He could hear me best, so I saved the really important prayers for Sunday morning.

I was sure that grasping Jesus' hand would make the picture—and my life—complete. *Seeing that happen in the picture,* I thought, *will serve as a symbolic assurance of our walk through life together.*

I was anxious to be in my private place of worship and prayer, with the lovely music all around me, in hopes I would see the picture again, so I could join Jesus on the mountain.

I raised my hands and closed my eyes and sang love songs to Jesus. Some of the songs were so sincere and emotionally empowered, I couldn't sing. There was so much love coming out of my heart, it got clogged in my throat, and I had to wait for it to come trickling out of my eyes.

The desire to be with Jesus in the picture was greater than the desire to see the picture itself, with all of the bright colors. I tried to set the stage in my mind. I formulated my thoughts, remembering every minute detail, trying to see myself approaching Jesus midway on the mountain and taking His hand. But the picture did not appear. I could have drawn it on a piece of paper, but I could not create the scene or the colors in my mind. All I could see was black space. The hour of worship was almost over, and I was very disappointed.

What have I done wrong? Why can't I do this, Jesus? I want so much to come to you on the mountain and be with you! I must! I can't live in this world all by myself, slumped down there by the tree! I must see the picture and join you on the mountain! Isn't that what you want me to do? Isn't that what you want, Jesus?

Nervously, I lifted my hands in the air, my head tilted back, and my heart seemed to twitch with panic. *Would He not appear again? Would He go on without me?*

Looking at the clock on the wall, I realized, *This will be the last song.* I dropped to the chair and took several deep breaths, feeling drained from efforts to see the picture again. With my hands folded in my lap and my head bowed, I closed my eyes and listened to the music, trying to relax, having given up hope of meeting Jesus on the mountain.

Then, I saw the green grass. It popped into my black space without any thought or preparation. The thick, soft grass and bright, colorful flowers were all around me. Slumped on the ground against the tree, I stared at the rocky path in front of me. My head turned, and I saw Jesus standing on the path at the foot of the mountain, not far away.

I felt my heart leap with joy when I saw Jesus so close, standing so tall! He lifted His arm with His hand open and extended it toward me where I was sitting in the picture, leaning against the tree.

I knew my desire was to get up quickly and run the short distance to Him, but I felt the shock of alarm when I realized I couldn't move! My arms were free, but my body would not budge. I watched myself pushing the ground with my hands, but I could not lift myself up! I was stuck to the ground and glued to the tree! He was standing there, waiting for me! I lifted both arms and reached toward Him as far as my body would bend. I was stretching and reaching for Him, crying out and beckoning Him.

Suddenly, the picture was gone. People were scuffling around me, taking the children to their Sunday school rooms, talking and laughing and hugging. I sat in the chair bewildered, limp and damp, breathless and utterly exhausted. *This,* I thought, *I do not understand at all!*

I could not comprehend the pastor's sermon. When finally the church service was over, I went home in a blurred fog. Bumpy lumps of fear lay on my skin all day. Confusion swirled in my mind. I was speechless and depressed.

By that evening, I was in a state of automatism, mechanically and automatically going through the motions to dress for the evening service. I had to go. I had to sing. I wanted to sing love songs to the King of kings. I would worship Him forever and ever; even if I had to do it slumped on the ground! Loving Jesus was in my veins. It was the first thing I did when I woke each morning. It was the only way I could live. I reminded myself that this was not the first strange occurrence since Jesus came into my life, and it probably would not be the last. I didn't understand what had happened in the picture, but I deduced there must be a reason. *Go forward,* my brain insisted. *Keep moving and keep loving Jesus, no matter what!*

I plodded through the thick fog and entered the sanctuary. Automatically, I went to the same chair, where I had sat at all of the worship services, including that morning, when I had anguished and struggled to get up and go to Jesus in that agonizing picture.

I sang, pushing words through my tight throat. Tears streamed down my face. I lifted my arms, giving everything in me. And I kept singing love songs to Jesus. When I could no longer read the words on the screen through the flow of tears, I rested my eyes and stared at the still, black sea. It was quiet and peaceful there. It was the place where I talked to Jesus.

I love you, Jesus, and I want to be with you. I know you know that. And, I know you love me, too. But there is so much I don't know. I'm confused right now. I don't understand why I could not get up. I don't understand why you wanted me to see that picture this morning. Teach me and show me what you want me to see. But don't ever leave me, please! Amen.

Soft, floating colors took shape in my mind, and I saw the green grass, just as before. I saw myself sitting on the ground, leaning against the rough, brown bark of the tree trunk. My arms were wrapped around bent knees, and my head was bowed down, my face buried in the round circle of arms. I saw myself crying, and I felt the loneliness in my heart.

Jesus came from behind the tree, walking on the rocky path. He stopped in front of me and looked down at my round, hunched back.

I could feel the warmth of His love, compassion and mercy, towering and enveloping me (just as I had felt it when I saw the light all around me in Rick's office), but the sad girl in the picture didn't know He was there. I wanted to shake her and tell her how close He was!

His tall, lean frame lowered to the ground, and He placed His hand on my arm. I saw my head slowly rise. He smiled a comforting, confident smile and gently laid His hand on the top of my head. I didn't see the grass or the flowers. There was no mountain in the background. I saw only His eyes, peacefully penetrating mine, and I heard the message that He wanted me to know: *You could not come to me, child, for you are heavy laden and weak. I have come to lift you up.*

I watched the moving picture as He took my hand in His. In one graceful, gliding movement, together we stood up. He gripped my hand securely and guided me onto the path. We walked together, hand in hand, on that narrow, rocky road. When we approached the foot of the mountain, we paused and gazed at the steep, jagged rocks ahead. I squeezed His hand tighter, and we started the climb. It was then that I noticed I was barefoot, too. I could see that Jesus was speaking to me, and I strained to hear the words. But the colors faded and the mountain dimmed, and the picture drifted away.

In the days and weeks ahead, I learned more about God from the Bible, which gave me a personal understanding of the symbols in the pictures.

The rough, brown bark of the tree trunk was the pain of my past. Many times, I had cried and cried, not knowing Jesus was by my side, watching over me. The soft, green grass was like the comfort zone of mediocrity. The tiny flowers peeking out of the grass were colorful temptations, attempting to lure me, to no avail. I was right where God wanted me to be. He wanted me to know that, without Jesus, I could do nothing. He showed me that I could not even get up and go to Him; though, all the while, He knew that was my heart's desire. Only Jesus could lift me up and set me free. He showed me that there would be difficult obstacles to cross along the way, but His promise was clear: if I would stay close to Him, He would lead me and guide me and teach me what I needed to know. Together, we would reach the heavenly place of everlasting life.

The lesson I learned that most deeply touched my heart was that Jesus came to me! Heavy laden I was, still trapped in addiction and destructive habits. I was as weak as a newborn baby against the dark spiritual forces that would have kept me glued to the tree. But He came to me and lifted me up, because He knew my heart.

I tried and tried but I never saw those pictures again. Yet, through all the years and tears since then, He has never left my side.

Chapter 5

For the record

The events described in chapters one through five transpired in 15 days. This chapter depicts significant events that happened simultaneously with the events described in the first four chapters from January 4th through 18th.

Wednesday, January 4, 1984
Spiritual Warfare

It was a Wednesday night when God first spoke to me saying, "There is a church across the street. Go there tomorrow."

For the record, Bette Vanderhoff, an elder's wife, later told me that someone had approached the microphone that Wednesday night, just before Pastor Tom was to begin his sermon. The Lord had given that person a message during the praise and worship service.

"Someone is in trouble," the person warned. "It's not someone here, in our midst, but someone nearby. I believe the Lord wants us to stop what we're doing and pray for someone in this neighborhood."

Unknown to me, two mighty armies were assembled when "I wondered if there really is such a thing as God."

The spiritual battle commenced when I began searching for hope and feeling despair. "Maybe? No! Possible? Not possible! Future? Fantasy!"

There were good angels and bad angels all around me in that dark living room, but there was also a battalion of normal human beings across the street engaged in spiritual warfare through prayer on behalf of someone they didn't even know.

The shepherd had left instructions with the flock to pray while He went to find one who was lost.

7 "I say to you that there will be more joy in heaven over one sinner who repents than over ninety-nine just persons who need no repentance." (Luke 15:7)

Jesus gave specific instruction to me also, perhaps through an angelic messenger, speaking words I could hear. "There is a church across the street. Go there tomorrow."

Their prayers of spiritual warfare on that Wednesday night also prepared their hearts to receive me—dirty and smelly, with no will to live and nothing to give. The appointed ones were ready, patient and kind, when I stepped through the door of that church the next day.

Thursday, January 5, 1984

Deliverance from sexual immorality

God drew me into the light of His love. In that light, God's loving-kindness led me to true repentance. It was more than saying, "I'm sorry, I'll try not to do that again." It was a significant turning point in my life. In one moment of time, my life was changed in the light of God's love!

I had been addicted to sexual stimulation since my first sexual encounter at age 18; although, it wasn't called "addiction" back then. It was a powerful need that I could not resist. It was an evil deception, playing havoc with a worthless self-esteem.

Even though "sex outside of marriage" was accepted among my acquaintances, as well as being a new national standard in the mid '60s known as The Sexual Revolution, it never felt right. Even though it felt wrong, I did it again and again, searching for love and approval through the performance of sex.

I believe it was during my experience in God's light that the emotional need and the physical compulsion for sex was removed from me. I had not specifically asked to be delivered from sexual addiction. I had cried, "Help me, please!" and God knew what I needed.

For the record, I was delivered from the bondages of fornication and sexual immorality when I was in God's light on January 5th, 1984; and, for seven years thereafter, sex was not a part of my life. Wanting it didn't enter my mind. I had male friends, but I was not inclined to have sexual relationships with them. They liked me, they loved me as a sister in Christ, and they respected me.

I had experienced a spiritual revelation of God's love for me in that aura of light, as well as an awakening awareness of sin. The physical, mental, emotional and spiritual transformation that occurred within me in the midst of God's light was a miracle, not of faith but of grace. Amazing grace!

For the record, I had a sexual relationship with a man in 1991, seven years after I had been saved. I could provide excuses by describing the extenuating circumstances which led to that intimate interlude, or I could blame the man involved, whom I will call Jack, or I could blame the devil. But the simple truth is: I let it happen. I slipped and fell.

Guess who was there to pick me up? I felt the presence of the Lord each time I undressed and laid down with Jack. Repeatedly, I felt the conviction of God's commands in my heart.

One evening, after a titillating, climaxing romp (which, by the way, felt very good to the flesh), Jack and I lay in the bed, quietly catching our breath. In a flatly factual tone of voice, I said, "Jesus is here, watching us. We should not be doing this. Not yet."

During the following week, Jack and I had several discussions about the sin of fornication, and we talked about waiting until we were married. I made the choice to wait, and Jack chose to leave. He fled like a scared rabbit, because the truth was revealed. Jack didn't love me. He had no intentions of marrying me. When finally I put God's Word first, before my own desire, the truth was exposed.

Again, I experienced Godly sorrow, knowing that the sin, which was hurting me, was hurting God.

I repented. Oh, how I repented with all of the Biblical knowledge in my head and love of God in my heart! Then, I allowed myself to receive God's forgiveness, and I thanked Him for that painful lesson. It was painful because I thought I was in love with Jack, but I had to let him go. Wanting God's will to be accomplished in my life and renewing my commitment to God was more powerful than the lure of lust and more important than feeling sorry for myself.

Throughout the next six years, until I was married at age 45, I did not have a sexual encounter, and I did not regret the discipline of abstinence. On two occasions, I was tempted within my mind (seeing and thinking but not touching), and I felt physical response to those temptations. A common term for that condition is "horny." That's eye-opening, considering the devil is usually depicted with horns on his head. I resisted the devil. I believe God stood by and watched, allowing those temptations without intervening, to test me. When I made the choice to say "No!" to sin and turn to God, He was right there to fight the spiritual battles for me, and Jesus wins every time.

With the exception of my downfall with Jack, I lived 13 years as a single woman, free and independent of compulsive promiscuity, thanks to the Lord Jesus Christ for taking the blinders off of my eyes and showing me the light of His love.

Friday, January 6, 1984

Forgiving is a choice

The day after I was saved, I put the Word of God into action when Robert attacked me. Call it "date rape," if that sounds more palatable, but it was a full-fledged, forced intention of rape. It was the strength of a man and the power of the devil against a weak woman who believed "there is power in the name of Jesus," and Jesus won! I believe there was an invisible angel in that bedroom doing the work of the Lord in response to my command to the devil, "In the name of Jesus! Get off of me!"

For the record, Robert married an older, wealthy woman one month later. They came to MY church, strategically sitting directly in front of me. She probably didn't know who I was, but Robert made sure I was aware of her. He made grand gestures, flaunting his expensive jewelry and new clothes, wrapping his arm around her shoulder and holding her hand. He proudly introduced her to the pastors and elders, bragging about her wealth and boasting of their new home in the richest part of town. The pastors and elders didn't know the real Robert, like I did.

I hated Robert! I found many scriptures in the Old Testament telling of bad things happening to our enemies, and I wished all of those bad things onto Robert. (I didn't know, at that time, that our enemies are not made of flesh and blood. Our enemies are "spiritual hosts of wickedness in the heavenly places," as stated in Ephesians 6:12.)

I told my confidant, Bette Vanderhoff, that I hated Robert and I wished he would go to another church, or I would have to find a different church.

Calmly and matter-of-factly, without condemnation, Bette replied, "You will have to get rid of the hate and forgive Robert."

Adamantly, I exploded. "There is no way I can forgive that man! He is evil! Can't you see? He's a liar and a hypocrite! He married that woman for her money! He is coming to this church only to irritate me! He deserves the worst possible punishment for everything he did to me!"

Still calm and matter-of-factly, without condemnation, Bette said, "Jesus can't live in a heart that's full of hate."

That statement stunned me. I was speechless. I knew I could not live without Jesus, but I also knew I could not forgive Robert. I felt my face turn white.

Bette led me to a chair. She opened her Bible and read several scriptures about forgiveness. The one that gripped my heart was in the first book of the New Testament.

14 "For if you forgive men their trespasses, your heavenly Father will also forgive you.

15 "But if you do not forgive men their trespasses, neither will your Father forgive your trespasses." (Matthew 6:14,15)

Tears filled my eyes. Feeling helpless and doomed, I whimpered, "I can't do it. I can't even imagine how I could forgive him. It's impossible."

"It's not impossible," Bette replied. She found a scripture in her Bible, then she handed the book to me, pointing to a verse (Luke 1:37), and she told me to read it out-loud.

"For with God nothing will be impossible."

"God will do the work to change your heart," she said, "if you are willing to let Him."

"Willing?" Truthfully, I asked, "How can I be willing, when that's not what I want? I think Robert should be punished!"

"God will be the judge of that," she said. "Your task is to be willing to forgive him, even if you don't want to, for your own sake. Otherwise, you will be imprisoned with hatred and unforgiveness. You must let Jesus break those chains, so you can be free. Truly free!"

"How?" I asked.

Bette turned the pages to another scripture in her Bible. The words were red, spoken by Jesus.

43 "You have heard that it was said, 'You shall love your neighbor and hate your enemy.'

44 "But I say to you, love your enemies, bless those who curse you, do good to those who hate you, and pray for those who spitefully use you and persecute you." (Matthew 5:43,44)

"Pray for Robert?" I asked, appalled, and sarcastically repeated, "You want me to pray for Robert?"

Bette smiled and said, "Jesus wants you to pray for Robert."

She waited, as I silently read that scripture again.

"Do you pray every night, before you go to sleep?" she asked.

I nodded my head up and down.

"Whatever you pray for yourself," she suggested, "pray the same request for Robert. Every night."

I took a deep breath and let the air flow out slowly, thinking that would be the hardest thing God could ever ask me to do.

"It's okay if you're not sincere in the beginning," Bette added. "God knows how you feel. You can't fool God!" she chuckled. "But your obedience will please Him, and He will reward you by turning something bad into something good!"

I reluctantly agreed to Bette's instruction. Every night in prayer, I told God the truth. I asked Him to forgive me for whatever deeds I had done or thoughts I had thought that day which may have made Him sad, and I asked Him to do the same for Robert. "Of course, you know I don't really want you to forgive Robert," I added, "but Bette said I should ask anyway." I asked God to protect me and to draw me closer to Him and to help me in many specific ways. Following each request, I asked God to do the same for Robert, always confessing that I didn't really mean it in my heart, and I knew that He knew it, "but Bette said I should ask."

This went on every night for three months.

On one particular night, I asked God to save Robert's soul and to give him a new life. The words I spoke startled me. It was an extra, special request that had come from somewhere in my heart, and I really meant it!

Forgiveness was complete, and I was free! Truly free!

The only way I can explain the relief, the peace, the genuine heart-felt hope for Robert's salvation is to say that a miracle happened in my heart, something only God could have done.

I continued praying for Robert for eight years. Not nightly but frequently. Whenever a thought or memory of Robert came to mind, I stopped whatever I was doing and sincerely prayed good things for him.

For the record, I received a phone call from Robert eight years later, in 1992. He was living in California. He had just met the Lord Jesus Christ, and he wanted to make amends to people he had hurt in the past. Sober and remorsefully, Robert asked me to forgive him for everything he had done to me. I assured Robert I had forgiven him long ago, and I told him I was happy about his salvation.

When I hung-up the phone, I smiled, and I could feel Jesus smiling, too, remembering the miracle that had happened in my heart eight years earlier—the miracle of forgiving someone who didn't deserve my forgiveness and the resulting desire deep in my heart for Robert to be saved. My persistent prayers for Robert's salvation had paid off!

As for the record in heaven, called The Book of Life, I believe Robert's name is in it. That's a miracle! And that's an example of why we should never give-up on the Lord! Just keep praying!

Sunday, January 8, 1984
Water Baptism

During the first Sunday evening worship service, I wanted to see Jesus, to be with Him, to know Him. I wanted it deeply in my heart, and it was all I could think about. God knew it, and He showed me a picture behind closed eyes. It was my first glimpse of Jesus standing on top of the mountain. It wasn't until later that I learned in the Bible about this kind of spiritual revelation, which is called a vision.

For the record, something else happened that night, too. At the end of the sermon, Pastor Tom announced that a water baptism would be performed after we were dismissed. Anyone who wanted to stay to witness and celebrate this blessed event was welcome. I didn't know what "water baptism" meant, but I was in a celebrating mood and eager to discover yet another one of God's secrets.

A large basin was full of water, about four feet deep. Curtis Newby, the associate pastor, approached the basin wearing a blue, short-sleeved, wrap-around, plastic dress that hung to his knees, and he was barefooted. He walked down a few steps to the center of the basin of water, carrying his Bible above his shoulder.

Along came a young man donned in the same type of blue dress, and he entered the water. Many people were crowded around the basin. I had to stand tall to see what was happening.

Curtis talked to the man in a quiet voice, and then loudly he said, "I baptize you in the name of the Father and the Son and the Holy Ghost." Swiftly and forcefully, Curtis put his hand on the man's head and dunked him under the water!

I was appalled! I had never seen this type of activity in a church, and I didn't know why Curtis had dunked that poor man! I held my breath for the man and watched intently.

When his head came out of the water, he was looking upward, smiling, with both arms extended high in the air, and he spoke like an infant, making sounds that made no sense. Noise came from every person in the room, a rumbling, mumbling sound, and I didn't know why they were making such a clamor.

I watched the people around me. They appeared to be exceedingly glad, clapping their hands, and several faces were wet with joyful tears.

Whatever this is, I thought, *it's something good that makes people happy! So happy, they're gibbering and can't talk right.*

Without a second thought, I raised one arm high in the air and waved it back and forth, like a schoolgirl wanting to be recognized by the teacher. I shouted, "I want to do this! Can I be next?"

All movement came to a halt. Everyone looked at me with perplexed expressions, as if they did not know how to respond to my outburst. I felt a hand on my forearm, pulling my body through the crowd. It was Rick. He guided me to a row of chairs away from the people.

"Do you know what Eric has done?" he asked.

"I know it must be something good. Everyone looks happy. So, I want to be dunked in the water, too!"

Rick smiled, and then composed himself in a serious manner. "Eric made a very important decision last week," he explained. "Eric decided to surrender his whole life, his past and his future, and start a new life with Jesus in complete control of it. When he went down into the water, the old man—the man he used to be—died and was buried. When he arose, he was resurrected to a new spiritual life, totally submitted to the Lord Jesus Christ. He thought about that seriously before making the decision, and he prepared himself for this appointed time to be baptized."

"I don't have to think about that very long," I exclaimed. "I hate the way I used to be, and I never want to be that way again! The sooner I get resurrected, the better!"

Rick studied my face, and then he looked beyond me where Curtis was standing, waiting for a sign from Rick. Curtis received a hand in the air, indicating the necessity of a little longer wait.

"Are you sure you are ready to lay down your life? Are you willing to give up everything?"

"Yes! I want to get rid of my old self, and I want to have a new life!" I was as excited as a child on Christmas morning.

"Okay," he said. "I'll get you a robe."

Rick glanced at Curtis and nodded his head up and down. I went to the ladies room, removed my clothes and put on the blue plastic dress.

When I was standing in lukewarm water, Curtis read some words from the Bible while I prepared myself, as if I was making a private wish before blowing out the candles on a birthday cake. *I want to have a whole new life with you, Jesus, and I'll do whatever you tell me to do.*

My head was pushed into the water. When I stood up, I felt God looking down upon me from high on the mountain, and I felt His joy! I felt new, untarnished and squeaky-clean.

How does clean feel? Fresh, shining, hollow, hungry, and ready to be filled! Like an old, grimy, sticky garbage can that was scoured with a huge S.O.S. pad, then sprayed with Lysol® to kill the germs and rinsed thoroughly to be used as a floral vase on God's window sill. For the first time in my life, I felt like a normal human being.

Far in the distance, I could faintly hear the rumbling, mumbling sounds and the clapping of hands. I was in my own private place, thanking Jesus for giving me a new life.

Water baptism, for me, was a public announcement of giving up my old life and an inner commitment to follow Jesus' way of life.

Wednesday, January 18, 1984

Prophecy and Baptism in the Holy Spirit

During the second Sunday evening worship service, Jesus came to me and lifted me up in the vision. His unconditional love for me and the supernatural power that He had shown me in that final vision melted my heart. I was like putty in God's hands, ready to be molded and shaped. I could hardly wait to get to church the following Wednesday evening.

The praise portion of the service was done. Pastor Tom approached the podium and introduced the guest preacher who would give the sermon.

Reverend Earl Roundtree, a short black man, wore a permanent smile that never left his face. Even when his loud voice, pounding fist and stomping feet spoke of doom or tragedy, his smile and wide-open eyes spoke of hope through it all.

The title of his message that evening was "The Revelation Of Knowing Who Jesus Christ Is." I still have the audio cassette tape of that sermon, so I am able to write exactly what he said. Otherwise, it would be an easy mistake to alter the title to be, "The Revelation of Knowing Jesus Christ." But that would be incorrect and incomplete. The man was telling us we need to know Who He Is.

He began with Matthew 16:13.

"Jesus asked His disciples, saying, 'Who do men say that I, the Son of Man, am?"

Reverend Roundtree held his Bible open in one hand and straightened his arm forward toward the people seated in the audience, and he asked, on Jesus' behalf, "Who do you say I am?"

I have kept the audio cassette all of these years because it contains a prophecy, a message of confirmation and encouragement, which the Lord spoke to me that night through Reverend Roundtree, right in the middle of his sermon.

The preacher was shouting, pacing back and forth on the wide platform and stopping at the podium just long enough to give it one hard hit. He had no trouble keeping our attention as he preached.

"God said He's going to build His Church, and He's looking for men and women willing to lay down their lives for the gospel's sake. He is giving us revelation of Himself. Unveiling, uncovering things you cannot see with the natural, and giving you a supernatural understanding of the Christ, the one that made all things and holds all things together by the word of His power. He is revealing Himself in you."

Suddenly, the preacher turned and looked directly at me. "Young lady, you will never be the same."

He stepped off the platform and walked toward me as he spoke. "He called you and laid His hands upon you for a purpose, and these are the beginning of days. Praise God!"

He reached for my hand and gently pulled me into the aisle. I stood next to him, and he placed one hand on my shoulder. His eyes were closed. Very seriously but constantly smiling, he continued with a loud voice, "He has given thee a hungerness for the Word of the Lord, and He shall give thee a quick understanding as you read His Word, and He shall change you from glory unto glory by the Spirit of the Lord. Be ye steadfast, unmovable in the things of thy God, and thy heart will rejoice and thy will dance in the presence of the Lord. For I shall make you as a sign in the land of the good things of the Lord. Oh, what I will do in thee and through thee! For ye shall be a gleaner in the field, telling others about our wonderful Savior."

Everyone clapped and hollered happily. I sat down, wondering how he had picked me out of a crowd of 300 people. Only thirty minutes earlier, Jesus had revealed Himself to me in the fourth vision. He had come to me and lifted me up. Jesus and I were on our way, hand in hand, up the mountain of life. And I knew, at least one part of what that man had said was true. From this night on, I would never be the same again.

When Reverend Roundtree's sermon was finished, Pastor Tom took a few minutes to spread the icing on the cake. He reiterated that spiritual revelation comes from the Holy Spirit. Pastor Tom had a way of mounting scripture upon scripture with quickening momentum, and he didn't have to wait long for the people to find the passages in the Bible, following along as he read the words, speeding on to the next scripture without stopping for interpretation.

Pastor Tom let God's Word speak for itself. Amazingly, everyone kept pace with his excitement.

A woman sitting next to me placed her Bible on my lap and found the scriptures as Pastor Tom announced them. We read silently, while Pastor Tom read them out loud. I was learning about the second baptism, as described in Mark 1:8, where John the Baptist said,

"I indeed baptized you with water, but [Jesus] will baptize you with the Holy Spirit."

The woman flipped the pages to Acts 1:5,8. In red words, Jesus said,

5 "... for John truly baptized with water, but you shall be baptized with the Holy Spirit not many days from now."

8 "But you shall receive power when the Holy Spirit has come upon you; and you shall be witnesses to Me in Jerusalem, and in all Judea and Samaria, and to the end of the earth."

We read Acts 19:1-6, which says,

1 "...Paul, having passed through the upper regions,
came to Ephesus. And finding some disciples 2 he said to
them, "Did you receive the Holy Spirit when you believed?"

So they said to him, "We have not so much as heard whether there is a Holy Spirit."

3 And he said to them, "Into what then were you baptized?"

So they said, "Into John's baptism."

[4] Then Paul said, "John indeed baptized with a baptism of repentance, saying to the people that they should believe on Him who would come after him, that is, on Christ Jesus."

[5] When they heard this, they were baptized in the name of the Lord Jesus.

[6] And when Paul had laid hands on them, the Holy Spirit came upon them, and they spoke with tongues and prophesied."

Then, we read Acts 2:4,

[4] "And they were all filled with the Holy Spirit and began to speak with other tongues, as the Spirit gave them utterance."

Further in the second chapter of Acts, we read versus 36 through 39,

[36] "Therefore let all the house of Israel know assuredly that God has made this Jesus, whom you crucified, both Lord and Christ."

[37] Now when they heard this, they were cut to the heart, and said to Peter and the rest of the apostles, "Men and brethren, what shall we do?"

[38] Then Peter said to them, "Repent, and let every one of you be baptized in the name of Jesus Christ for the remission of sins; and you shall receive the gift of the Holy Spirit.

[39] "For the promise is to you and to your children, and to all who are afar off, as many as the Lord our God will call."

Next, we read Ephesians 3:16-19, where Paul was praying for the people:

16 that He would grant you, according to the riches of His glory, to be strengthened with might through His Spirit in the inner man,
17 that Christ may dwell in your hearts through faith; that you, being rooted and grounded in love,
18 may be able to comprehend with all the saints what *is* the width and length and depth and height—
19 to know the love of Christ which passes knowledge; that you may be filled with all the fullness of God.

Suddenly, I understood why I had felt hollow and hungry last Sunday night, like a clean vase ready to be filled with God's fragrant flowers! And the people mumbling words that made no sense must have been speaking in "other tongues." Being baptized in the Holy Spirit instantly made perfect sense to me, and I did not want to miss a single good thing that God could give to me.

I was the first person to step forward when Pastor Tom invited us to come and pray and ask Jesus to fill us with the Holy Spirit, that we might truly know Who He Is. All of the elders were standing by the altar, ready to pray with anyone who wanted more of God. I went to the first row of chairs where Rick was sitting and took his hand. Without asking him, I pulled him to the steps leading to the platform. Others were kneeling at the altar, but Rick and I sat on the carpeted steps.

"I want to be baptized in the Holy Spirit," I declared. "What should I do? What should I say to get the Holy Spirit?"

"All you have to do is ask," he replied.

Rick opened his Bible and read a scripture to me, quoting Jesus:

9 "So I say to you: Ask and it will be given to you; seek and you will find; knock and the door will be opened to you.
10 For everyone who asks receives; the one who seeks finds; and to the one who knocks, the door will be opened.
11 "Which of you fathers, if your son asks for a fish, will give him a snake instead?
12 Or if he asks for an egg, will give him a scorpion?
13 If you then, though you are evil, know how to give good gifts to your children, how much more will your Father in heaven give the Holy Spirit to those who ask him!" (Luke 11:9-13)

Rick closed his Bible and said, "In your own words, from your own heart, ask God to fill you with His Holy Spirit, and He will do it."

I prayed out loud. Rick placed one of his hands on my shoulder and mumbled quietly.

When my prayer was finished, I lifted my head and looked at Rick, anticipating further instruction.

He simply said, "Speak."

I asked, "What should I say-yordia-konda-la-moriada-nahasada-see-onda-leeoka."

Purposely, I closed my mouth. My eyes probably appeared as big and round as golf balls, glaring questions at Rick but afraid to open my mouth to ask them. I did not know what had come out of my own mouth, sounding like my own voice, but I knew I had not formed the words on my own accord. It seemed the strange sounds gushed from my stomach and spilled out of my mouth. My face felt hot and flushed.

"Go ahead," Rick prompted me to speak more.

The words had startled me and left me stunned. My mouth remained closed in defiance and refusal, uncertain of what would come out. My body was rigid and stiff.

Rick patted my back and smiled, "You don't have to do it right now. But you have been given the gift of tongues. If you will use the new language that God has given you, you will become more comfortable with it."

Rick explained that the new words were to be used for prayer. "It is the Holy Spirit in you, praying to the Father on your behalf," he said. "When your own words are not enough to express what's in your heart, the Holy Spirit knows exactly what to pray." Rick opened his Bible and said, "You see, it's written right here."

"… the Spirit also helps in our weaknesses. For we do not know what we should pray for as we ought, but the Spirit Himself makes intercession for us with groanings which cannot be uttered." (Romans 8:26)

Driving home that evening, I felt overwhelmed, knowing that God loved me. Knowing He was big enough to make all the bad sins go away. Knowing there was power and victory in the name of Jesus. Knowing I was squeaky-clean, embarking on a whole new life with Jesus. Knowing that Jesus Christ cared about me enough to come to me and lift me off the ground and walk with me up the mountain. Knowing my life would never be the same again, that the mysteries of God would be revealed to me and more happiness than I could contain would abound in the days ahead. Knowing the Holy Spirit was in me, that He had filled me, just as a hand fills the empty space inside of a glove, and I wanted to cut holes at the finger tips and let some of it out. My entire being was full of gratitude. In the privacy of my car, I started to thank God out loud, but the Holy Spirit took over. He knew exactly what to say. I let the foreign words come out, and they flowed freely and fluently all the way home. I had never before known such peace!

Anyone can make-up strange sounding words. And, there is a peaceful, calming effect when a person clears their mind completely and does not think of anything that makes sense. People of the Hindu religion claim the attainment of a peaceful state of meditation from repeating mantras. Even hypnotism is achieved by clearing the mind's thoughts. But ***nothing*** can be compared with the power of the Holy Spirit's prayer to our Father in heaven.

The Holy Spirit is our mediator. I became convinced of that one day soon after I received my baptism in the Holy Spirit. I was driving my car on a neighborhood street, approaching a busy intersection, and I was speaking my prayer language out loud. One block before the intersection, the pronunciation of the words suddenly changed dramatically, and the sounds were identifiably Chinese. Having lived in Hawaii for four years, I had heard Chinese people speak their native tongue on a few occasions, but I did not know a single word of the language. Even if I had attempted to pretend to speak Chinese, my words would have been awkward, choppy and clumsy. The words coming out of me that day were free-flowing and graceful, spoken with a tone of confidence, authority and authenticity.

When finally the traffic cleared, I turned onto the main street of the intersection. One block further, I noticed a Chinese restaurant. The volume of my voice was turned up, almost shouting a Chinese dialect.

Two blocks beyond the restaurant, the Chinese sounds quit, and my own prayer language that God had given to me resumed.

I believe the Holy Spirit was praying through me for someone in that place who needed God's help.

On other occasions, while praying in the Spirit, I have received wisdom, comfort, encouragement and guidance. I received those benefits with clear, concise understanding, although I was speaking words that I didn't understand at all. Praying in the Spirit is faith in action. The benefits are miraculous by our human standards, but they are God's way of giving us what we need—through the Holy Spirit.

Many mainline Christian denominations acknowledge the Holy Spirit in their affirmation of faith but deny the operation of some of the gifts of the Holy Spirit in this day and age. Yet, Jesus warned us, saying,

28 "Assuredly, I say to you, all sins will be forgiven the sons of men, and whatever blasphemies they may utter;

29 but he who blasphemes against the Holy Spirit never has forgiveness, but is subject to eternal condemnation" (Mark 3:28,29)

God is the giver of spiritual gifts. Not every Christian receives every spiritual gift. The Apostle Paul gives explanation of the distribution and use of spiritual gifts in I Corinthians 12:4-11 and I Corinthians, chapter 14.

I am immensely thankful for the Biblical teaching I received at Wichita Christian Center. When the Bible lessons with Rick were completed, my counseling sessions were concluded. My heavenly Father began raising His baby girl. Jesus became my mentor and my best friend. The Holy Spirit was the big brother I never had when I struggled alone. He gave me spiritual understanding and taught me truths that I would have never known in the natural, limited, human mind.

The family of God

For the record, I had excellent teachers in the family of God.

Pastor Tom Garrelts' expression of faith was inspirational. His elated enthusiasm and excitement about the exalted, triumphant Lordship of Jesus Christ was contagious. His wife, Jeanne Garrelts, affected me the way the Statute of Liberty greets foreigners who have never stepped on American soil. She was a worship leader, standing on Holy ground, and she demonstrated the freedom to worship the Lord God Almighty with her whole heart and all of her mind, which was to me an invitation to come closer to the throne of God.

Elton McMillan, a scholar of the Old Testament, a humble man with an entertaining sense of humor, correlated complicated Biblical history into practical application for the people of today.

Bill and Bette Vanderhoff welcomed me into their home, into their lives and into their hearts. Even when they smelled alcohol on my breath or cigarette smoke in my hair, they didn't put me down but lifted me up with prayer and encouragement. Their response to the multitude of inquiries that I hammered upon them was living, breathing evidence that there's no such thing as a dumb question.

Associate Pastor Curtis Newby and his wife, Grace, always seemed to understand how I felt. It wasn't pity or sympathy. It seemed to be empathy. Perhaps their understanding came from God's omniscient (all knowing) heart.

Jim Baker was a prominent businessman. Yet, Jim and his wife, Jan, never hesitated to speak the truth to anyone who needed Jesus, in the church or in the business world.

I had never before known people like this—people who were unashamed, unafraid, uninhibited to tell it like it really is. Some people consider that kind of evangelism to be wild, uncontrolled emotionalism. In truth, it was pure love. In the power of that kind of love emerged freedom from fear and condemnation. Jesus commanded us all to go forth with that kind of love, spreading the gospel throughout the world. Even in my hometown.

Finally, I had learned the truth at "the church across the street," and I was no longer afraid. There is no human means of justly thanking those people and others for treating me as Jesus would have, if He was still in human form.

Until she is greeted at the gates of heaven, Jackie Gough won't truly know what it meant to me to be welcomed into God's House with open arms and with the love of Christ. Her patience, kindness and bear hugs were anointed!

There are no words in the English language profound enough to express my gratitude to Rick for boldly and lovingly acting on his spiritual awareness of my needs and for patiently feeding me Holy milk.

We have traveled in various directions since those days. All I can do is thank God for those people and carry on their legacy of love as "a gleaner in the field, telling others about our wonderful Savior."

Chapter 6

Total surrender and deliverance from alcoholism

From the moment I asked Jesus to be my Lord and Savior, life was much easier, but I had a lot to learn from God, and He didn't shove all of it down my throat in one gulp. Becoming a Christian happened instantly, but being a Christian is a lifestyle. Salvation of my soul from eternal hell happened in one split second, but salvation from deep-rooted sin is sometimes a process, step by step, and God's timing is perfect!

During the first seven months of my new Christian life, God and I were busy enough working on things like cleaning-up my language, forgiving Robert, and establishing a new client base for my freelance copywriting business. I was getting to know Jesus and learning how to live in peace, in love, in joy. I was very happy! I didn't know I was addicted to alcohol.

My first alcoholic drink was a Salty Dog, Vodka in grapefruit juice. I was 16, at Susie's slumber party, when we raided the cupboard where her parents kept their booze.

The next morning, my girlfriends were laughing about how clever we were to sneak out of Susie's bedroom window to go to Kenny's party and then what a great job we did TPing the trees in Johnny's yard. "Did I fall asleep," I asked, "and you did all of that without me?" No. They told me I had a lot of fun and I was the life of the party! But I didn't remember any of it.

I'd had a blackout. Sixteen years later I learned that a blackout is a symptom of alcoholism. It's a period of time in which one functions (consciously talking, walking, even driving) but doesn't remember any of it. It didn't take years of progressive drinking for me to become addicted. Since I had a blackout with that first drink, I was addicted right then and there, and I could hardly wait to have more.

I was a daily drinker throughout those 16 years. It was part of my daily routine, like brushing my teeth three times a day. I drank a little in the morning, some at noon and every night.

My older sister, Bobbie, had seen the worst of my depression and my drinking habit. Bobbie claims she had talked to me many times about my abusive drinking, but I don't remember even one conversation until the day God enhanced my hearing, loud and clear.

I stopped at Bobbie's house while running errands and I was surprised to find her home instead of at work. I just wanted to grab a beer, and then I would be on my way.

"Do you know what time it is?" she asked.

"Nine o'clock."

"Nine o'clock in the morning and you are drinking a beer!" she accused.

"So?"

"I've had it! If you don't talk to someone, a professional counselor, today …"

"Today?"

"Today! By five o'clock …"

"I don't need a counselor."

"I … am … serious!" Her words were slowly spoken, articulate and commanding. "If you don't see a professional counselor by five o'clock today, I am going to commit you to an alcoholism treatment center. Tonight!"

She was serious, and I knew she would do it. My whole world stopped. For the first time, I heard every word she said, and I was stunned.

Many years of experience as a people-pleaser came to my rescue. "Okay," I agreed. "I'll see a counselor, but one day doesn't give me much time to find a good one."

"Five o'clock," she said in a low voice, and then she walked out of the house and went to work.

I called the county mental health facility because their services were free, but the receptionist said, "I can't fit you in today."

When I told her about my sister's threat, she told me to come, wait in the reception area, and she would somehow squeeze me in.

I waited in that reception room for five long hours with two thoughts fighting in my mind. *Could I really be an alcoholic? No way!*

At four o'clock, I met John. He explained that the counselor who specializes in alcoholism could not accept new patients because her schedule was full. His was, too, but he offered a clever alternative.

"If you don't think you are an alcoholic, prove it. Stop drinking. But if you need a drink or even want a drink, I suggest you go to an AA meeting."

The first part of his advice sounded better than the latter. I would "prove" to Bobbie that I was not an alcoholic.

That evening, I gave John's business card to Bobbie to show her that I'd seen a counselor, and I reported John's advice. I would simply stop drinking. No problem.

The next day, in my small office at the Parklane Office Park complex, I was typing copy for a client's newsletter and ran into writer's block. I went to my file cabinet, opened the bottom drawer, reached underneath the stack of papers and lifted the buried bottle of scotch. I poured some into a glass and drank several quick gulps before remembering, *I'm not supposed to drink!*

The following day, I had a drink at a restaurant during lunch. *One little drink isn't a big deal,* I convinced myself.

Each day was the same. I found plenty of excuses to have one little drink, then another and another. Each drink, I promised myself, would be my last.

After several more days of broken promises, I wasn't just thinking of John's suggestion. I was no longer trying to prove it to Bobbie. I had to know for myself that I could quit. I threw away the scotch bottle from the bottom drawer of my file cabinet and the one under the front seat of my car and the bottle under my bed at my mother's house, where I was living.

The next morning, two weeks after my appointment with John, I was sitting in my car in the parking lot of a restaurant at 10 o'clock, waiting for it to open for lunch at 11 o'clock. Then I could have a drink at the bar.

How did I get here? I wondered. I could not remember driving to the restaurant, and I didn't know how long I had been sitting in the parking lot, but I knew I could not wait a whole hour. I tried to think of a bar that would be open and whispered desperately, "Where can I go?"

If you need a drink or even want a drink, I suggest you go to an AA meeting. John's voice was as clear as if he was speaking to me from the back seat of my car.

I knew where to go. I had passed by that closed door in the Parklane complex many times and had read the words on the door sign, "Alcoholics Anonymous." I had seen the schedule of meeting times on the door: "Daily at Noon, 7:00 p.m., 10:00 p.m."

I had two hours to kill until noon. I drove to the highway, heading out of town, and I had a serious conversation with God.

"I don't want to go to that place, Lord. Those people can't help me! They're just a bunch of sorry drunks! I've seen those people, wobbling and stumbling, living in alleys! I'm not like that! What's wrong with me, Lord? Why can't I stop drinking?"

God was silent. I felt His presence and I knew He had heard me, but He didn't answer.

I was fighting mad, arguing out loud as the speedometer climbed to 80, ranting and shouting excuses to the Lord when suddenly I realized … God was not listening. He was gone! I knew it, just as surely as I knew when God was with me. What a difference! I felt empty, alone, going nowhere.

I stopped my car on the side of the highway and closed my eyes. "Jesus, forgive me for shouting at you, and please hear my prayer. I need you. I don't know what to do. If you won't help me, I'll have to go to that place! I'll have to go to those people for help! Oh, God, couldn't this be just between you and me? Lord? Are you listening?"

He didn't answer. I could not feel the Lord's presence. I felt abandoned.

At noon, when I opened that door and walked into that room, I felt defeated and lifeless. I could hear my heart pounding, but I was numb. The meeting had already started. I sat in a chair, staring at the floor. I couldn't look at the people in the circle of chairs. Someone was talking but I didn't listen.

I looked up and saw posters and signs on the wall, directly in front of me. One read, "Let Go and Let God." Another read like a prayer: "God, grant me the serenity to accept the things I cannot change, courage to change the things I can, and wisdom to know the difference." Another poster was a long list of twelve sentences:

1. "We admitted we were powerless over alcohol—that our lives had become unmanageable.
2. Came to believe that a power greater than ourselves could restore us to sanity.
3. Made a decision to turn our will and our lives over to the care of God as we understood Him."

Suddenly, I realized, *He's here! God is right here in this room!* I felt God's sigh of approval when I finally got the message. *This is where He wants me to be!* Sunlight shone through the window, and the room was very bright!

I looked at each person sitting in the circle. Several men were dressed in suits and ties, some in jeans and T-shirts. The women wore dresses, suits, slacks, jeans. They were regular people, and some of them were smiling! When one person finished talking, the next person in the circle spoke. Each person began by saying their first name, then that awful statement, "I am an alcoholic." Some of them said, "I'm an alcoholic and drug addict."

Soon, it would be my turn! I squirmed in my chair. When the person next to me finished talking, all eyes were on me. Nervously, I introduced myself.

"My name is Jo and … well, I don't know … I mean … I sort of suspect that … maybe I might be an alcoholic. I'll just listen, if that's okay."

The next woman spoke without hesitation. "I'm Hazel and I'm an alcoholic."

I was glad she took the attention off of me. I listened to what she said. I liked her voice and her smile. She seemed calm and strong and wise.

When the meeting was over, Hazel asked if I wanted to have a sponsor. "A sponsor is someone who has been in the program for at least a year," she explained. "Someone you can call if you have questions or just want to talk."

I had a lot of questions, so I asked Hazel to be my sponsor. She was an artist and worked in her home, so I could call her any time of day or night. She gave me her phone number, written on a scrap of paper, and a firm command, "Don't drink, and come back tomorrow."

I didn't drink that afternoon, and I attended the seven o'clock meeting that evening. I was there the next day at noon and again at the evening meeting. I was amazed to hear those people talking about their feelings and what it was like when they first came to AA. They were speaking my own thoughts and feelings. I was encouraged, and I hadn't had a drink for two days.

The third day, though, was the most frightening day of my life. I woke drenched in perspiration. I was terribly nauseous and dizzy. Mother and Bobbie had gone to our lake house in Missouri, and I was alone in my mother's house.

I sat at the kitchen table and pressed my fingers on my throbbing forehead. The air was thick and dry. I took deep breaths, but I could not get enough oxygen. My body was trembling, and sweat dripped off my chin. I gasped and wheezed and I could hear my throat sucking air. Each breath was shorter and quicker. I grabbed a small brown grocery sack from the cupboard and put it over my mouth, concentrating on each breath. *In, slowly. Out, slowly. In, slowly. Out, slowly.* Finally I could breathe without the sack, but I was dizzy and wobbling.

I need a drink! I rubbed wet hands together and wiped them up and down my thighs. *No, I can't have a drink. Stay calm,* I instructed myself. *Think!*

Breathing heavily, I stared at the floor, trying to focus my vision on the pattern of the linoleum tiles. *I'll go to the meeting at noon. Yes! I've got to get to that meeting!*

I glanced at the clock on the kitchen wall. It was 8:30. *I'll never make it until noon.* I thought I would faint soon. *I need a doctor! I need some Valium or something to calm me down!* My heart was beating so fast, I thought it would explode. *I've got to do something!*

I found the piece of paper in my purse with Hazel's name and phone number. Trembling, I lifted the handle from the wall phone and saw, on the round dial, a huge, black, hairy spider! I threw the phone handle at the wall base and jumped backward, convulsing, too scared to scream.

Gasping short, quick breaths of hot air, I stumbled to the wet bar in the den, like an infant learning to walk. *I've got to have a drink!*

Cocktail glasses were lined up neatly in a row on the top shelf. I fell to the floor and stretched both arms into the bottom shelf, pushing soda pop cans aside and knocking them over. There were so many pop cans! Then, I felt the short, slender shape, a pint of bourbon. I hated the taste of bourbon, but at that moment, I didn't care what it was. Any booze would do.

I stood too quickly and nearly fainted but held onto the edge of the bar for balance. I grabbed a short cocktail glass from the top shelf and forced one foot in front of the other, step by step, stumbling toward the kitchen. My body was convulsing and I was afraid I would fall before I got there. If I fell, I was afraid I would not have the strength to get up.

Sitting at the kitchen table, I saw at my side a large, blurred bulk of something moving slowly into the den. It looked like a lion. I didn't care. I stared at the bottle and the empty glass in front of me. My arms were jerking violently, and my hands were shaking so wildly that the bourbon spilled on the table as I poured it into the glass.

I wrapped both hands around the glass and slowly lifted it. The strong smell of bourbon made my stomach reflex, and vomit filled my mouth. I spit the foul taste on the floor.

Oh, God, I know I shouldn't do this, but I have to! I'm going to die if I don't drink it!

The small scrap of paper with Hazel's phone number was lying on the table next to my arm, partially soaked with bourbon. Breathing heavily, I stared at it and then glanced at the phone on the wall. The spider was gone. I blinked hard twice and tried to focus my vision on the phone to make sure it was gone. I wanted to get up and go to the phone, but my body was heavy. My head was whirling. I couldn't move.

A hand gripped my upper arm and lifted me out of the chair. The grip was secure, leading me to the phone a few steps from the table. I didn't know who it was, and I wasn't curious about whom it was. I had to talk to Hazel! She would know what to do.

The blurred lion stalked slowly from the den, through the dining room, into the living room. He was moving away, so I ignored him, reminding myself, *If a mean dog thinks you're not afraid of him, he'll leave you alone and won't hurt you.*

I put my finger in a hole and turned the dial until it stopped. Each turn of the dial was more difficult. Finally, I heard her voice say, "Hello."

"Hazel, I need help!"

"Jo?"

"Help me, Hazel! I'm dying! I know I am dying!"

"Where are you, Jo? Tell me where you are."

"My mother's house. There's a lion in the living room! And spiders! I can't breathe!"

"Calm down, Jo. I know it feels awful. It sounds like you're going through withdrawal."

"Hazel, I need you to call an ambulance!"

"Okay, Jo, you might need to go to a hospital. But first, listen to me. A lot of people go through this. You're going to be okay, I promise. Can you hear me?"

"Yes, I can hear you."

"Don't drink, Jo. No matter what. Don't drink anything but water. You'll probably vomit, but that's okay. You need to get the toxic chemicals out of your system, and it might take two or three days …"

"I really need a drink, Hazel!"

"I know you think you need a drink, but don't do it! Stay on the phone and listen to me. Have you done step three?" she asked.

"What?"

"Step three. Have you done step three?"

"Wha … what's step three?"

"In the Blue Book. The twelve steps, remember?"

"Oh, yeah, but I can't remember step three."

Pronouncing each word slowly and clearly, Hazel said, "We made a decision to turn our will and our lives over to the care of God as we understood Him. That's step three. Have you done that?"

"Of course! I'm a Christian!"

"Listen carefully to the words, Jo. We made a ***decision*** to turn our ***will*** and our ***lives*** over to the ***care*** of ***God***. Have you really done that?"

I didn't answer.

"That means your whole life, Jo. Whether you live or die, you've got to be in God's hands."

"Okay, Hazel. Okay, I'll do it."

"Good. I want you to call me back if you're feeling worse. Will you?"

"Yes, thanks. Thanks very much."

I hung-up the phone, but I knew I wouldn't be calling her back because I seriously thought I was going to die.

I stumbled to the kitchen table, repeating Hazel's warning, "Whether I live or die, I've got to make sure my life is in God's hands!"

I picked up the glass and the bottle of bourbon and went to the kitchen sink. My legs were stiff, like stilts. My body was jerking and shaking. Bourbon spilled out of the glass, down the drain, and then I tipped the bottle in the sink until it was empty.

I went back to the table and my hands came together, my fingers entwined, squeezing so hard that my knuckles were white. I didn't care where the lion was, and I wasn't afraid. I was about to turn my whole life, what was left of it, over to God. I closed my eyes and prayed out loud.

"I'm letting go, Lord, right here and now. Nothing else matters. I am putting my whole life in your hands, Jesus. It's not much, but here I am. All yours. I surrender my will, all of my body, my mind and my heart to you. If I die here today, please take me to heaven. But if you don't want me to die yet, you are going to have to take charge. I can't manage my life anymore. I've been saying I belong to you, Jesus, but I don't think I have ever meant it as much as I do right now."

That prayer came from every fiber in my body, deep within my soul, and permeated the room.

I sensed the presence of the Lord, like never before! I felt a warm hand covering my left shoulder. It was Jesus standing beside me, blessing me and receiving me into His loving care. The power of His love was so strong, my head fell upon my folded arms on the table and I cried. They were thankful tears. Whether I lived or died, I was sure that my life was in His hands.

When I lifted my head, I was alone. Jesus was not at my side. The lion was gone. I took a deep breath, and I was surprised that the air went in smoothly and came out easily. My body was not twitching and shaking but perfectly still. My hands were calm, and my skin was dry. I wasn't dizzy or nauseous. I was solid, whole and well. The powerful need to have a drink was gone!

It was July 25, 1984, when I walked into that first AA meeting. That was the day I quit drinking, but I celebrate my anniversary of sobriety on July 27th because that was the day Jesus Christ delivered me from the physical, mental, emotional and spiritual addiction of alcohol. I haven't had nor wanted a drink since then.

I will never forget the emptiness and loneliness I felt when I was driving on the highway and thought God had abandoned me. When Jesus was hanging dead on that cross two thousand years ago, it seemed the Father had abandoned His beloved Son—but not for long! He had a plan that would set His people free! He had a plan for me, too. God wanted me to go to that meeting and to understand the importance of Step Three, and He knew Hazel would help.

In my prayer on the highway, I asked God, "Couldn't this be just between you and me?" Totally surrendering my life to God was indeed a personal decision in the privacy of my mother's kitchen, just between God and me. But first, Jesus took a brick out of my wall so I could see that there were people out there in the world I could trust. He sent me to a place where I could learn about this disease called alcoholism. A place where I could help people, too.

My private, personal relationship with Jesus was no longer my own. It was extended to others in many ways. That's how God works sometimes—through people.

God works in wondrous ways! I don't think it was a coincidence that I had rented office space at the Parklane complex, where the AA group was located. I think Jesus was leading me and guiding me, even before I knew it.

Who gripped my arm and guided me to the phone? I think that was a guardian angel. But it was Jesus Christ standing beside me with His hand on my shoulder. When I made that commitment to surrender my whole life to Jesus, He touched me and healed me—not in a vision or a dream but in real life at my mother's kitchen table.

Chapter 7

God really does hear prayer

I was standing in line at the cashier counter of a bookstore and became keenly aware of the woman standing in front of me. I am not a short woman, but I felt short, standing next to her. The straight, vertical lines of her navy-blue skirt and suit jacket, high heels and stiff posture emphasized her height. Her hair was short and fashionably styled, which drew attention to her long, slender neck and gold earrings. Her nails were perfectly manicured, a pretty shade of coral, and the diamond on her left hand was enormous. I could see she was a woman of means and wealth, but I could not ignore the feeling that something was terribly wrong. Her demeanor was tense and anxious. I discerned a feeling of desperation.

When she shifted her position, I was shocked to see the book she was holding, ready to buy. I recognized the title and knew it was a product of the New Age religion.

My immediate reaction was to tell the Lord. Silently, with wide-open eyes glaring at the book, I hailed His attention. *Look, God! She's going to buy that book! If she's searching for answers, Jesus, please don't let her be misled!*

She moved to the counter and paid the cashier. I wanted to stop her and tell her she shouldn't buy that book, but I didn't.

She lifted her package and headed toward the door to leave. I felt as if I was standing by and watching a thief jab a knife into an innocent bystander's heart, and I wasn't doing anything to help her.

Before leaving, the woman stopped at a display of greeting cards, near the exit door, and thumbed through several cards. Silently, I urged the cashier to hurry with my purchase, and I beckoned the Lord's guidance.

What should I do, Lord? What should I say? She'll think I'm weird if I tell her that book is wrong for her. How can I help her understand something so important with only a few words? Help me, Lord!

The woman walked through the exit door and into the parking lot. The cashier gave me my receipt, and I stepped away from the counter. Without a hint of direction from the Lord, I stood there, speechless, watching the woman walk away. I took a deep breath and released a groan of disappointment, resigned to failure out of hesitance, nervousness and fear of her response.

I went to my car, which was parked closest to the store. She was still walking between parked cars. I sat in my car motionless, feeling like a coward. In the silence of sadness for her and remorse for not saying something that might have helped her, I heard a voice.

"Tell her you are an alcoholic."

It startled me! I looked around. I even looked in the back seat of my car to see who was there. Then I realized it was the voice of God! The words were as clear and audibly understandable as if a person sitting in the back seat had spoken them. I was stunned. I didn't breathe, and I didn't move a muscle.

Like an echo in the air, I heard the voice again. "Go and tell her you're an alcoholic."

I glanced across the parking lot and saw the woman standing next to a car, searching for keys in her purse. There was no time to devise a plan. I got out of my car and started toward hers. Thoughts swarmed my mind. *Tell her I'm an alcoholic? What does my being an alcoholic have to do with her reading that book?* Suddenly it occurred to me that her husband might be an alcoholic. *But she is not going to find the right answers in that book!* The plan was clear. I had to convince her to return that book!

"Excuse me," I called from a short distance.

She looked at me with darting eyes. I tried to smile.

"I was standing behind you at the check-out line, and I noticed that book you bought."

Her face was hard. Her eyes squinted with piercing accusations of my intrusion.

I cleared my throat and continued. "I thought you might like to know … in your best interest, of course … it's not a good book, and I don't think you should read it."

Her back straightened. Her tall stature towered over me, and she looked down at me with indignation. "A good friend of mine recommended this book," she said.

"Oh." I tried so hard to smile. "I'm sure your friend meant well, but maybe your friend doesn't know either."

I could see the wall go up between us, in the expression on her face. She put her hand into her purse and retrieved the keys, turned her back to me and unlocked the car door.

I knew I had blown it and she wouldn't listen to a word I would say now. *Dear Lord, what I should I do?*

Tell her you are an alcoholic!

The voice was loud and strong within me. Goose bumps crawled on my arms and a shiver ran up and down my back.

She got into her car. Just before she closed the door, the words came out of my mouth.

"Please, wait. You see, I am an alcoholic. I guess I should say I was an alcoholic, but if I would drink again, I certainly would be an alcoholic in the present tense." I chuckled, trying to lighten a heavy subject. I stood there, waiting for a response, knowing I looked and sounded as ridiculous as I felt.

As she reached for the door handle, I moved out of the way. She shut the door, but my eyes remained fixed on her, and she stared at me from inside the car. Slowly, she lowered the window. Her glaring eyes were daring me to explain myself.

"This might sound strange," I said, "but, God told me to come over here and tell you that I am an alcoholic." I grinned sheepishly and shrugged my shoulders, opening my hands defensively. "I don't know why He wanted me to tell you that." The words were coming easily, so I continued. "I tried to stop drinking, but I couldn't do it. Jesus helped me. He did for me what no human, especially myself, could have done."

Even though she was glaring at me, a genuine smile finally spread wide on my face. "Well, anyhow, I just wanted to tell you that you're not going to find Jesus in that book. I'm sorry, if I disturbed you."

I turned and walked away feeling relieved, yet bewildered, wondering what purpose would be accomplished from this strange encounter. I was more than halfway between her car and mine when the woman shouted, "Wait!"

I turned around and saw her getting out of her car. Slowly, I walked toward her, praying earnestly that God would come to my rescue and take charge of this awkward situation.

Within a few feet, I could see that the hard lines on her face were now soft and sagging. Her mouth was down turned and her chin was trembling. "I think I am an alcoholic," she said. Her head cocked slightly to one side. The words surprised even herself. "I've never said that out loud, but I know I am … an alcoholic." Her voice was strained, and the words barely squeaked out. "I can't quit drinking, and I don't know what to do!"

My heart collapsed from a flood of memories. "I know," I spoke softly. "I felt that way, too. It's frightening."

Tears welled in her eyes. Her fingers pressed hard against her lips.

"God knows, too," I said gently and absolutely. "He knows how you're feeling, and He wants to help you."

Holding her breath, unable to speak, she was about to explode. I stepped forward to embrace her, carefully placing my arms around her rigid body. She moved, as if to resist, but to my surprise, she freed her arms to wrap them around me. She leaned heavily on me and cried. Sobbing and gasping, she murmured some words that I couldn't understand. It didn't matter what she was saying at that moment. I held her, and I could feel God's love flowing through me into her.

Finally, her trembling body settled, and the weight was almost more than I could balance. I asked if she would like to sit in her car and talk for a while.

We sat silently for a moment and then she spoke. "I have never believed that there really is a God, but I didn't know what else to do. One night, last week, I actually got down on my knees, and I prayed. But the next morning I had the shakes so badly, I had to have a drink! Then another and another. I couldn't go to work. I've lost my job! And my husband …" Her eyes squinted tightly shut, but the tears were not contained. They flowed down her cheeks in streams. She covered her face with both hands.

Gently, I pulled her hands down and guided her chin to look at me. The contortions of shame on her face relaxed when her eyes met mine and she saw my smile. It was a confident smile, even in the midst of her pain.

"God is real," I said. "He heard your prayer and sent help! Why else would a stranger approach you, as I did, and tell you that I'm an alcoholic? God sent me because I know how frightened you are and how hopeless it seems. I felt that way, too. But I also know everything will be alright for you because Jesus loves you. He knows exactly where you are, and He can provide a way out of this maze of fear. He did for me."

Her chest rose as she breathed in deeply, and her sigh of relief was audible. Staring at folded hands in her lap, she whispered, "It must be true. God must have heard my prayer."

The fullness of joy I felt in that moment of truth filled my entire body! I was overflowing with gratitude for the Lord's victory! Inside, I was gleefully singing, *Hallelujah! Praise the Lord!* I wanted to leap through the parking lot, shouting the good news, *Look what the Lord has done!*

Somehow, though, I restrained myself, knowing I had to stay calm and keep the momentum going. I smiled and waited a moment, letting the realization of God's love soak into her soul.

We talked a while more. I told her about Jesus' birth, death and resurrection. When she said she was ready to repent, I held her hands and we prayed. I was nervous, knowing this was the most important prayer of her entire life, and I wanted to say the words just right for her, as Rick had done for me. She thanked Jesus for being her Savior and asked Him to be her Lord forever and ever. When we finished, I realized the words we had spoken didn't have to be precisely perfect because we had sent them in the name of Jesus, and the words had come from her heart.

The marvelous journey for her was just beginning! She shared her testimony in church and at support group meetings with enthusiasm and absolute faith. "If there's any doubt," she would say, "let me tell you the truth. God really does hear your prayers!"

What a privilege and an honor it was for me to be part of God's plan that day when He called her into His Kingdom.

Chapter 8

The faceless were left behind

One year after Jesus delivered me from alcoholism, I started the Wichita Chapter of Sunrise Ministries, a Christ-centered support group for alcoholics and their family members. A few weeks after the ministry was up and running, God gave me a vision which instilled in me an enduring sense of compassion for lost, empty souls.

The vision transformed me to another place. It was like a dream, but I was not asleep. I was walking in a field. Wheat was swaying all around me, as far as I could see. It wasn't tall and ready for harvest but about a foot high. It looked like a golden sea on a breezy day, rippling lazily and sparkling in the sunshine. There were no buildings or people; only wheat and the horizon, the blue sky and white, fluffy clouds. It was a lovely day! The wind was blowing just enough to move my bangs and wipe my brow.

I noticed the clouds moving in the sky. I thought that was curious because the wind was gentle and soft. More clouds came in the sky, swirling and stirring. I had always enjoyed finding shapes in the clouds, like a rabbit or a car or a bike. I studied the strange movement of the swirling puffs, and I saw a face. It was a man's face.

Far ahead, near the horizon, I saw a cluster of people walking in the wheat, traveling the same direction as I was. I glanced to my left and saw a few people, and to my right, a few more. Everyone was walking toward the horizon. Amazingly, people appeared here and there, too many to count. As we walked, more and more people joined the march, as if we were all going to the same place, toward the horizon together. Hundreds, then thousands of people were strolling in the swaying wheat with a purpose and destination, but we were not in a rush. It was such a lovely day.

I glanced up and was shocked to see the clouds twirling in the sky, rolling over and over, colliding with each other. The clouds in the middle of the sky began to stir most violently. The clouds on the left slowly moved further to the left in the sky, and the clouds on the right slowly moved further to the right, like a curtain opening slowly on a stage.

I looked at the many people nearby. They didn't seem to notice the sky, and they weren't very friendly. Everyone seemed to be minding their own business, walking toward the horizon. I kept walking, too, and didn't bother anyone with conversation. I would have liked to visit with someone along the way, but no one seemed to be in the mood to chat.

When I looked up again, the clouds in the middle were shaped like the face I had seen. It was a man's face, but it had long hair. I was astonished to see wide shoulders emerge, and the shape began to grow. I saw arms and a chest, elbows and hands. Taller and taller it grew! I watched intently, walking forward, and I became concerned.

Suddenly, a bolt of shock ran through my heart and mind. I recognized the loving face. *It's **Jesus** way up there!*

"Look!" I shouted and pointed upward, "**Jesus** is in the sky!"

I was thrilled to see my Lord! I wanted to run and jump and clap my hands with joy! But they were just meandering. Their stroll was tired and slow.

"Don't you see?" I shouted. "It's **Jesus** in the sky! Look up! Look up! The Lord's right there! **Jesus** is alive!"

But no one looked. They didn't hear. They didn't seem to care. Step by step, they all kept pace, trodding unaware.

It made me mad, and it made me sad. I didn't understand. *They must not know the Lord God, or they wouldn't be so blah!*

I looked again, His shape complete, solid, strong and big! He moved toward us, inch by inch, growing very large.

Then, it hit me ... Jesus ... is coming in the clouds!

Oh, my gosh! This is it! This is really it! He's coming now to get us! To take us home! Now they'll see! They've got to see! They've got to hear and know! He's King of kings and Lord of lords. But only the saved will go.

I ran to a man nearby, shook his arm and exclaimed, "That's **Jesus** up there! He's coming to get us! Just those who believe. Do you know He's the Lord? Are you saved and redeemed? Can you not even hear what I am trying to say?"

The man didn't budge, except his feet. He just kept walking through the wheat.

I ran to a woman and lifted her chin. "Look up! Don't you see? That's the Lord Jesus Christ, and He loves you and me! He paid for all of your dreadful sins, and He wants to take you home!"

She didn't flinch or crack a smile. She just kept walking, all the while.

I ran to some children and lifted one up, and I smiled as I pointed my arm. "That's Jesus up there! He loves little kids. He knows just how you feel. He knows your name, and He has a plan specifically for you! Will you say yes? Just say okay! Oh, please, just give it a try! It's so important! No time to lose! Say 'yes' to the Lord right now!"

The kids were blank. Not a smile on a face. No expression of yea or nay.

I took a big breath and looked around for someone else to tell. My body was light, so very light. I was lifted up from hell.

"Oh, no, dear Lord! Not just yet! Wait! I can't go yet! So many here, I've got to tell! So many more to get!"

An inch, then two, I was going up, but they were walking still.

"Oh, dear God! Wait! Please wait! Give us another day! These people are blind! They can't see you! We need more time to pray!"

As I went up, others, too, were drifting up and up. But very few were going up. So many left behind!

I looked down, five feet away, and saw the worst disgrace! The people trodding in the wheat had heads but not a face! Ears were on the sides of heads and hair on top. But eyes, noses, mouths were gone! They didn't have a face!

"Oh, God!" I turned and looked at Him, as I drifted higher. "We can't leave so many, and no one with a face! They can't see or smell or eat. They'll starve in that awful place!"

He spoke to me lovingly but painfully, too. "I told you, child, I'd come again. I said it would be soon. You had the time. You had the chance. But many still are strewn."

"Oh, Lord," I cried with sorry tears, "I want to go with you ... but those poor souls will never have another chance to come! I'm sorry, Lord. So sorry, Lord. There's more I could have done."

My heart was torn in halves, for I was on my way, and I was very grateful to be glory bound this day. But there, way down below, was a herd of faceless souls. I didn't know their names. I didn't know their woes. My broken heart was aching for those faceless, nameless people. Millions of them, trillions! Forgotten and forsaken!

I knew there was nothing I could do about it now. But last month or last week, I could have somehow.

I knew there was no way I could have made a dent in that massive crowd of people who refused to repent. But one or two, ten or twelve, maybe even more, might have eyes to see and ears to hear. I could have done much more!

Nearer and nearer, I rose to meet my Lord. He stretched His arm and pulled me close to snuggle at His side. His arm wrapped around me, as we watched the earth below.

I'd never known such heaviness, such painful, piercing sorrow! The sadness and the loss I felt was now not just my own. I looked at Jesus' face and saw a tear for them below.

I knew He was hurting, too. He loved them all so much! He died for them, such horrid pain, hanging on the cross! He fought for them and won the war, so they could be free! So they could live happily throughout eternity!

"But now it's time for us to go," Jesus said to me. "They had the time. They had the chance. They chose to stay below."

The power of that experience truly changed my perception. I no longer saw drunks walk through the door of Sunrise Ministries' support group meetings. I saw beautiful faces that simply needed the love of Jesus Christ. Some accepted what Jesus had done for them. Some didn't. Some were saved and healed. Some weren't. It's a choice each person must make. Tomorrow might be too late.

Chapter 9

A prayer for healing

In the Bible, Jesus told us to cast out demons, to pray for our enemies and forgive them, to lay hands on sick people for healing. Those exhortations are related. If there was no evil or sin in the world, there would be no sickness.

I was speaking to a demon when I looked at Robert's yellow eyes and told him to get off of me (chapter 3). I prayed for Robert and truly forgave him for everything he had done to me, and both of us were spiritually healed (chapter 5). I have laid my hands on sick people, and they were healed. It wasn't me, who performed those miracles. It was God, responding to my faith and obedience.

There have been other occasions when I have laid my hands on sick people, and they were not healed. I don't tell God what to do. I ask and He answers according to His will—not mine. God's will for me and for all of His children is good and righteous and perfect, even when we don't agree with it or understand it.

The key to accomplishing God's will is to let Him do it. He might or He might not utilize me and my faith to accomplish His will. That's why I say the "Serenity Prayer" every day.

"God, grant me the serenity to accept the things I cannot change, courage to change the things I can, and wisdom to know the difference."

Sometimes I repeat the Serenity Prayer several times within a day or within an hour or in a critical moment, because I don't know God's will in every circumstance.

Especially when there is a need for healing for myself or for others, I always apply the "Serenity Prayer." Following are three good examples.

God, grant me the Serenity to accept the things I cannot change.

The year was 1987, three years after I was saved. I was working more than full-time in Sunrise Ministries, without pay, and I worked part-time as a freelance copywriter, barely making enough money to manage living expenses.

I didn't have dental insurance, but I went to the dentist once each year to have my teeth cleaned. The dental hygienist always took x-rays, searching for expensive cavities to fill, and poked my gums and gave me lectures about flossing.

My dentist told me I had holes in my gums, far exceeding normal, acceptable depth. He explained that virtually every adult has some measure of receding gums. A measure of three or four on the depth scale is common and not considered critical. I had a few holes that measured three or four, but I had ten holes that measured six to ten on the depth scale. My dentist warned that if I did not get this problem fixed, it would not be long before my teeth would fall out, and buying dentures would cost more than repairing my gums and saving my teeth. He recommended a procedure to remedy the problem, and the treatment would cost 75 dollars for each hole.

I quickly multiplied 75 dollars times 10 holes and exclaimed, "Seven-hundred-and-fifty dollars?"

What he was proposing was so preposterously unaffordable, it was laughable!

He didn't think it was funny. He told me to seriously think about it, and he suggested getting a second opinion, so I would realize the severity of my condition.

I did get a second opinion. A friend of a friend of mine was a dental hygienist, and she recommended the dentist where she worked. That dentist confirmed the diagnosis, not knowing that his was a second opinion. He measured the same depth in all ten areas of my gums. He strongly recommended the treatments and offered to perform the procedures for the same cost, $750.

I went home discouraged, knowing I would have to have my gums repaired soon or face the inevitable prognosis later. The notion of losing my teeth and wearing dentures at age 35 was inconceivable. Yet, my mother had to get a full set of dentures when she was 40 years young. I decided

I had better think seriously about where I would find 750 dollars. Each idea was sarcastically comical.

Get a loan at a bank? That was humorous. I had no collateral.

Make monthly payments to the dentist? That was funny, imagining the dentist agreeing to a five-year payment plan.

Borrow the money from my mother or a friend? That was just as funny as paying the dentist over five years; that is, if I could eat less and scrounge an extra twelve dollars and fifty cents from my food budget each month for five years.

My monthly budget never stretched as far in real life as it did on paper. I lived on faith. If I was going to find 750 dollars from my income, it would have to be a miracle. The thought of another miracle made me smile.

I also thought about trying to acquire new clients in my freelance copywriting business to make more money. The time required to service those additional clients, though, would reduce my time spent in the ministry, and that was not funny. More people were coming each week to the Sunrise Ministries support group meetings, and many of them asked for individual counseling. My schedule was already stretched as far as humanly possible.

Having found no solution in my brain, I gave this problem to God.

"I need some serenity, Lord, to accept the things I cannot change. I can't solve this problem, so I am putting it in Your hands. I am going to let go of it and trust that You will solve it. I honestly don't care how You choose to do it. If You want me to go through the dental procedures, I will trust that You will provide the funds to proceed in that direction. You provide for all of my needs!

"On the other hand, if You want to heal my gums … please do! I know You are able to restore my gums! That would be the easiest route for me.

"Either way, Lord, I will be grateful, and I will give You the glory. It's entirely in Your hands, and I will wait for your guidance."

There was nothing more I could do. That being done, I referred to my long list of "Things To Do" for that day and proceeded in performing the duties of my work. I had confidence and faith in Jesus and an abundance of serenity.

What happened henceforth sounds irresponsible, but it's true. I completely forgot about the holes in my gums! The weeks and months ahead were jam-packed with responsibilities. Worrying about my gums was not my responsibility, because I had given that one to God.

It wasn't until I turned the page on my calendar one year later and saw the reminder notation, "annual dental exam," that I remembered I'd had deep holes in my gums a year earlier. I wondered if God had healed my gums. I assumed He had, because the cost of 750 dollars had not presented itself, and my teeth had not fallen out.

My dentist poked my gums and wrote the measurements on my chart. There were only three holes, and the deepest hole measured 3 on the scale.

"You must have had the scaling treatments done somewhere else," he said, with his hand in my mouth. "Whoever did it, did a good job."

He removed his hand, and I smiled. "Yes, He's very good."

"Who did you have do it?" he asked, with a tone of resentment.

"God." I replied, still smiling.

He didn't believe me at first, but I finally convinced him that I had not employed a dentist to fix my gums.

"If that's true," he said, "this is a miracle!"

"Yes, it is," I exclaimed.

News of God's miracle spread throughout that office within seconds. Dental hygienists, assistants, clerical personnel and patients came into the room. I was glad my dentist stayed in the room with me to personally and professionally verify that my gums had been in critical condition but now were restored to nearly perfect health, "supposedly without dental work," he exclaimed.

"Jesus did the work!" I added.

God, grant me the Courage to change the things I can.

While driving to church, I started to turn my head to see if a car was in the left lane, before changing lanes. I felt a sharp pain in my neck, and I could not turn my head far enough to see the blind spot in the left lane.

I drove into the first parking lot driveway on the right side of the road and stopped my car. Again, I attempted to turn my head toward my left shoulder, but it stopped and wouldn't move further left. The pain in my neck was boggling!

Looking straight ahead, I felt no pain. I could turn my head toward my right shoulder without pain. But each time I attempted to turn my head leftward, it would stop, as if my neck was jammed, and the pain was excruciating!

I was not far from my church, so I drove the distance, being careful to keep my head straight.

When I arrived at church, I went to the pre-service prayer room where many people were praying for God's presence to be at the praise and worship service. I couldn't wait until the church service was finished, when the pastors and elders would pray for anyone who had prayer requests at the altar. I announced my immediate need for prayer.

Everyone gathered around me, placing their hands on me, and prayed for God's healing power. Hands were on my head, shoulders, arms, all over my back. Pastor Tom poured oil on his palm and cupped his large hand around the back of my neck. Some people knelt on the floor and placed their hands on my thighs and calves, even my feet. Those who couldn't reach me through the crowd touched the shoulder of someone who was touching me. All of us were linked together in agreement of faith. Everyone prayed audibly. Some were shouting. Others whispered. I heard many people speaking their prayer language in other tongues. Some were speaking scriptures about healing, putting the living Word of God into action. Others quoted scriptures in spiritual warfare, commanding the evil influence to be gone from my neck.

When their prayers were finished, I turned my head easily toward my left shoulder, and I felt no pain. Everyone rejoiced! I thanked the people for their prayers, and I knelt to thank Jesus for healing my neck.

Driving home from church on that Sunday night, it happened again. My head would not move leftward, and the pain brought tears to my eyes. I thought about driving directly to the emergency room at the nearest hospital. The only other option was to pray.

Sincerely, I spoke the Serenity Prayer audibly in my car. As soon as I finished saying, "courage to change the things I can," I heard a song on my praise tape. I finished the prayer and turned the volume up on the cassette player. I sang the words, "Be strong and take courage. Do not fear or be dismayed, for the One who lives within you will be strong in you today."

Suddenly, I thought of a scripture.

"But He was wounded for our transgressions, He was bruised for our iniquities; The chastisement for our peace was upon Him, And by His stripes we are healed." (Isaiah 53:5)

I turned the volume of the cassette player down to a low hum. Several scriptures popped into my mind, and I spoke each scripture out loud.

"The Lord is my rock, and my fortress, and my deliverer; my God, my strength, in whom I will trust." (Psalms 18:2)

"I can do all things through Christ who strengthens me." (Philippians 4:13 NKJ)

"Behold, I give unto you power to tread on serpents and scorpions, and over all the power of the enemy; and nothing shall by any means hurt you." (Luke 10:19)

"Resist the devil, and he will flee from you." (James 4:7)

"He who is in you is greater than he who is in the world." (I John 4:4)

My voice grew louder and stronger with conviction. When I shouted, "In the name of Jesus, get thee behind me, Satan!" ... the pain was gone! I turned my head left and right, up and down, and I felt no pain.

I turned the volume of the cassette player up, and sang along with voices on the tape, "The Lord liveth, and blessed be my rock, and let the God of my salvation be exalted!" All the way home, I sang happily and gratefully, giving all of the glory and honor to my Lord Jesus Christ.

The next morning, I was still full and overflowing with gratitude, turning my head easily either direction.

By mid-morning, though, the sharp pain reoccurred when my head started to turn toward my left side. Something was in the back of my neck, blocking my head from turning left.

It was debilitating and serious enough to see a doctor. I called to make an appointment, but the doctor's schedule was full that day. My appointment was at 4:00 on Tuesday, the following day.

Meanwhile, I praised Jesus for healing my neck (even though it hurt), and I rebuked the devil. Each time I did that, the pain went away, and I could freely move my head!

The next day, I described to the doctor the piercing pain and inability to move my head toward my left shoulder. At the time of my appointment, though, the ailment was not present. The doctor told me to come back, without needing an appointment, if it happens again.

It happened again and again, every two or three days over the next three weeks. Each time it happened, I worshipped Jesus in songs, and I quoted scriptures in spiritual warfare, and the pain instantly went away. Since that process was working well, I didn't go back to the doctor.

One day, I was talking on the phone when it happened, and I screamed! The sudden pain, when I turned my head, was unbearable! I asked my friend to wait a moment. I laid the phone handle down and began shouting.

"You are the King of kings and Lord of lords, Jesus. You are the great 'I AM,' the Prince of peace, the bright morning star! Your Word says,

14 "These will make war with the Lamb, and the Lamb will overcome them, for He is Lord of lords and King of kings; and those who are with Him are called, chosen, and faithful." (Revelation 17:14)

5 "Who is he who overcomes the world, but he who believes that Jesus is the Son of God?" (I John 5:5)

"I believe that You, Jesus, are the one and only begotten Son of God, conceived not of man but of the Holy Spirit in the womb of a virgin! And I am an overcomer, according to Your Word. You said in Your Word, Lord Jesus,

24 "Therefore I say to you, whatever things you ask when you pray, believe that you receive them, and you will have them." (Mark 11:24)

I spoke out loud, "I have received healing in my neck, and it is mine!

10 "The thief does not come except to steal, and to kill, and to destroy." (John 10:10)

I proclaimed, "I will not let the evil one take a single blessing from me!

"My faith has healed me, and I will go in peace."

(Luke 8:48)

"Get thee behind me, Satan, in the holy, precious name of Jesus!"

That scriptural, spiritual recital took only a couple of minutes. The pain was gone. I returned to the phone and cheerfully said, "Okay, thanks for waiting. What were you saying?"

"What was that about?" she asked.

"I have a pain in my neck," I explained. "God healed it, but it keeps sneaking back. I refuse to give-in to it, though. When I stand firm in my belief that Jesus healed me, the pain goes away."

"Wow! How long has this been going on?" she asked.

"It's been three weeks," I replied.

"Shouldn't you see a doctor?"

"I did, but I had commanded the pain to be gone before my appointment, and it was gone. He couldn't treat something that wasn't there."

"Will you have to shout it away for the rest of your life?"

"No," I chuckled. "But I will 'shout it away' for as long as it takes, until it gives up and quits pestering me."

"It?"

"Whatever 'it' is, it's not from God. It's evil."

One week later, I suddenly realized that a whole week had passed with no occurrence of pain in my neck. It was obvious to me that the demons had given-up.

The Bible says,

"They overcame him [the devil] by the blood of the Lamb, and by the word of their testimony;" (Revelation 12:11).

After my testimony to my friend on the phone, there was no more pain!

"He sent his word and healed them." (Psalms 107:20)

The scriptures I spoke, to retain my miracle of healing, are God's words. It was the power of God's Word that gave me "the courage to change the things I can."

God, grant me the Wisdom to know the difference.

This story is out of chronological order, but it's worth telling. I have to take you back to my first year of sobriety, before I became a leader of Sunrise Ministries.

The topic of discussion at an AA meeting was, "Alcohol is our enemy."

When it was my turn to speak, I told the group that "Satan is my enemy. Alcohol is merely a weapon that the devil uses to hurt people, particularly those of us who are addicted to alcohol."

My exhortation intrigued a woman, who approached me when the meeting was over.

"My name is Izie," she said. "Short for Isabel."

She asked me if I would go to her home and tell her and her family more about the devil and God. She gave me directions to her house, and I went there that evening.

Izie was a black, recovering alcoholic married to a white, practicing alcoholic named Hank. Izie introduced me to

Hank and their teenage daughter of mixed race, Debbie. She was a senior in high school.

It didn't take long to realize why Izie had wanted me to go to her home. She had been unsuccessful in coercing Hank to attend an AA meeting. Hank was looped (very drunk). He sat at the kitchen table, drinking rum from the bottle, while Izie, Debbie and I sat in the adjoining living room. Very softly, Izie asked me to speak loudly enough for Hank to hear.

Hank was a large man, taller than six foot, and heavy. Izie was short and petite. Debbie was my height, five-foot-six-inches, and slender. Too slender, I thought. She seemed nervous, stuffing potato chips into her mouth before the previous bunch was chewed and swallowed.

Izie kept glancing at Hank, then looking at me, and I saw fear in her eyes. Izie's and Debbie's nervousness was making me nervous, suspecting that Hank was a violent drunk, and I wondered if we three women were in danger.

Izie and Debbie asked specific questions about the devil, and I answered some of their questions from the perspective of my own personal experiences. They didn't have a Bible, but I had brought mine. I showed them scriptures in reference to their questions, as well as I could. I had to look in the Concordance to find some of the scriptures, but Izie and Debbie were patient, all the while keeping an eye on Hank. They were like sponges, soaking up every drop of the Word of God that spilled out of my mouth.

Each time either of them glanced at Hank, they suddenly thought of another question about the devil or about the power of God.

I wanted to get out of that house, but I wanted to take Izie and Debbie with me. I was close to suggesting a hot fudge sundae at Dairy Queen®, when we heard a loud thump. All three of us simultaneously jerked, and our bodies jumped three inches in the air. Hank's head had landed on the kitchen table. He was out cold. Each of us drew in a slow, deep breath and exhaled a sigh of relief. Izie grinned embarrassingly and said, "He has a hard head."

Three hours had passed quickly. During that time, I had led Izie and Debbie in a prayer of repentance and salvation. Both of them received Jesus as their Lord and Savior, as if their lives depended on it that very night, with no time to spare.

Hank was snoring on the kitchen table when I got up to leave. Izie asked me to come again, at a time when Hank would be sober. I suggested a Saturday morning, knowing that Hank would probably have a hang-over, yet maybe I could talk to him before he would have time to get drunk. I told Izie I would bring one the guys from AA with me, and she agreed. Saturday was four days away.

Two nights later, at nine o'clock, Debbie called me on the phone. Izie was in the Intensive Care Unit at a hospital. Debbie asked me to come quickly to pray for her mother. I arrived at the hospital twenty minutes later.

"They don't know what's wrong with her," Debbie gasped, with tears streaming down her cheeks. "She's in a coma, and the doctors said she probably won't make it through the night! Even with the life support system, her vital signs are bad. She is deteriorating so quickly! What's happening?" she screamed. "Why would God let this happen? You said we were saved! You said God loves us!"

I felt slapped in the face with questions that I didn't know how to answer. Life or death was hanging in the air. I wished I had called an elder to meet me at the hospital, so I could hear and learn the answers, too. I didn't know what to say.

Debbie was hysterical. I felt like a fish out of water. Hank was quietly sitting in a corner of the ICU waiting room with his face in his hands and his elbows resting on his knees.

I asked Debbie quietly, "Did your dad hurt your mother?"

"No, no! Daddy had nothing to do with this. Mother just collapsed! We don't know what's wrong with her!" Debbie was frantic.

"Come and sit down, Debbie. Can I get you a soda or water?"

"No! I want you to pray! Don't you understand? My mother is dying!"

I led Debbie to a comfortable chair, and I sat next to her. I knew I was stalling, but I didn't know what to pray. I wanted to urge Debbie to have courage and faith to believe that God would miraculously heal her mother, but I didn't even have the courage to say that. For all I knew, God might be taking Izie to heaven that very night, and that would be something we would have to accept. I needed wisdom to know how to pray. I needed guidance! I needed experience! I needed help!

Hank lifted his head. His face was soaked with tears. He looked at me and softly said, "Pray for Izie, please."

Debbie ran to her father and wrapped her arms around him and cried with him. I watched them hugging each other tightly, rocking back and forth in each other's arms.

Silently and urgently, I said the Serenity Prayer. *God, grant us the Serenity to accept the things we cannot change … Courage to change the things we can … and Wisdom to know the difference.*

I knelt in front of them and put one hand on Hank's arm and my other hand on Debbie's knee.

Hank spoke with a quivering voice, "Tell God that I'll quit drinking. I will, I promise! I'll quit if He will save Izie's life!"

The love in Hank's voice was more truthful and powerful than the promise of a drunk. I saw a different man than the one I had feared two nights earlier. He was a great big teddy bear, gentle and loving, broken and falling apart.

"Listen to me, both of you." I paused and gave them a moment to wipe the tears off of their faces. "I can't bargain with God! And I can't promise you that God is going to snap his fingers and zap Izie out of this coma! Only God knows what will happen tonight and tomorrow and the next day. But I can tell you this … Izie's life is already saved. Her soul is saved, and she belongs to Jesus Christ."

They stared at me with blank, unsatisfied expressions.

"I know you want a miracle right now. So do I! But first, we need to let go of Izie and put her in God's hands, for her sake! Let her sit on her Father's lap. Let Jesus speak to her."

Hank and Debbie looked deeply into my eyes, curiously.

"All I am asking you to do is trust God. Whether Izie lives or dies. Let God have the reigns. No bargains. No promises. Just let go, and put her safely and securely in God's hands. Can you do that?"

"Yes," Debbie said, absolutely. Hank nodded his head in agreement.

"Okay. Let's go in there and do that."

We walked to Izie's bedside. The sight of tubes running in and out and around her jolted me, and I almost lost my balance. I took Debbie's hand in mine, and we stood side by side. Hank stood on the other side of the bed. Debbie reached across her mother's frail body and held her father's hand. I put my right hand on Izie's chest and closed my eyes.

"Dear Lord Jesus, we lift Izie up to You, and we ask, Father, that Your will be done in Izie's life."

I could not think of any other words. I repeated, "May Your will be done, Lord." Again, I said, "Not ours, but Your will be done, Almighty God."

I opened my eyes and saw Debbie glaring at me, as if to say, "Is that all you're going to pray?"

My response was a confident smile, because I felt the Holy Spirit rising within me. My left palm was warm against Debbie's hand, and my right hand, on Izie's chest, was hot! I knew I had prayed all that needed to be said.

I sat with Debbie and Hank in the waiting room. A doctor spoke to us, with less hope than earlier.

"Don't lose hope," I said. "We have prayed a very powerful prayer! Now, we have to wait on the Lord and trust Him."

At midnight, Debbie urged me to go home. She promised to call me and keep me apprised of Izie's condition.

Four hours later, the phone on my bedside table rang and jerked me out of sleep. Before picking up the receiver, I thought, *It's over now.* Tears filled my eyes. I scooted up and leaned against the headboard of my bed and cleared my throat. "Hello," I spoke somberly.

I heard Debbie gasping and sniffling. I waited, trying to think of what I would say to her.

"He did it!" she shouted. "God let her live!" The shrill of her voice vibrated like an echo in a canyon.

I sat straight up, pressing the receiver hard against my ear.

"It was God's will!" she shouted. "Just as you prayed! She is sitting up in bed, wide awake, and she's hungry! The doctors are amazed! All of the nurses are freaked-out! None of them understand what happened. But I know! It was God's will for my mother to live!"

I rushed to the hospital to witness and rejoice in the Lord's majesty. Izie was released to go home later that morning.

The doctors did not know why Izie's body had shut down. Their only explanation for her recovery was, "a miracle."

A nurse in the Intensive Care Unit told me that she had recently rededicated her life to Jesus in prayer. She had asked Jesus, in that prayer, to reveal Himself to her and give her some sort of sign to let her know that He had heard her prayer. She believed that miracle was for her, too.

Hank joined Izie at the AA meetings and quit drinking. Izie believes that God performed that miracle for Hank. She had asked God to use her to get Hank's attention, so Hank would truly know that God is real. She told me that she would have given anything, even her life, for her husband to be well.

Debbie confessed her illness of anorexia and her serious thoughts, previously, of committing suicide. She claimed her mother's miracle for herself as well. It saved her life.

It was a miracle for me, too. God gave me the wisdom to get out of the way and let Him do His will. He didn't need a long-winded, fancy prayer. It was short and simple, but it was a powerful prayer, "Thy will be done."

Chapter 10

Unconditional love

I was a three-year-old Christian and had been sober for three years, ministering to alcoholics through Sunrise Ministries support group meetings when I discovered that even Christians are human, and humans are not perfect. For a performance-oriented perfectionist like me, it was a hard lesson to accept.

It was Tuesday when I received the first phone call. All day Monday and Tuesday I had been sitting on my couch, still shocked that my parents (my pastor and the elders) were getting divorced it seemed, and my church family was split. I didn't want to talk to anyone. After nine rings, I thought it might be my mother, calling to console me. I thought I should try to act like I was okay to relieve her burden of worrying about me. Begrudgingly, I picked up the receiver.

The man on the phone introduced himself as Pastor Collins. He was calling from Halstead, a small town about 45 miles from Wichita. He said he had heard about Sunrise Ministries on the radio, and he had gotten my name and phone number from the public service announcement. He was calling to ask for my help concerning a woman named Jackie.

"She's 25," he said, "and she's been addicted to alcohol and drugs since she was 16. I have spent months ministering to her and praying for her, but she has not responded. She has two small children, but she can't take care of them. Her husband has admitted her to three alcoholism treatment centers, and none of them were successful."

"Excuse me, Pastor …"

"Please, let me explain the background," he continued, hurriedly. "Three months ago, my wife and I made arrangements with Jackie's husband to move Jackie into our home. We have committed ourselves to caring for her full-time. We've been feeding her, bathing and dressing her for three months."

I slumped low on the couch and crossed my legs on the coffee table, knowing it would be a long background. *Everyone has a long background,* I reminded myself.

"My congregation has been faithfully interceding for her around the clock through our prayer chain. We have laid hands on her many times and rebuked the devil. She has not been drinking or smoking since she has been living with us, but she has not uttered a single word. She seems to be in a trance. She walks where we lead her, and she eats when we feed her, but she won't speak. She has not spoken a word in three months. I think she is at least obsessed, if not possessed, by the devil."

"After all you have done, Pastor Collins, what do you think I can do?"

"I don't know," he answered honestly, "but I believe God will lead you. Will you meet with Jackie and talk to her?"

I purposely coughed and cleared my throat, delaying my answer. He would be the first person to hear my decision, and it wasn't easy to say. "I'm sorry, Pastor Collins. I am resigning from the ministry. I am struggling through a difficult problem of my own right now, and I can't help you."

"You may be her last chance. We have no other alternative but to put her in a mental institution."

"I'm sorry."

"Will you …"

"No, I can't! I don't mean to sound disrespectful, pastor, but I have to go now."

I wasn't moved by his dilemma. Putting that woman in professional hands at a mental institution was probably the right thing to do. There was nothing I could do to help her. I was in the midst of a living nightmare, and I felt like I was in a trance. My body, mind and heart were numb.

The nightmare had begun two days earlier at the Sunday evening church service. I had gotten to church an hour late. The praise and worship service had ended. Pastor Tom was praying as I entered the sanctuary, so I stood by the rear door, waiting for an appropriate moment to find a seat.

There wasn't an appropriate moment. Pastor Tom announced to the congregation that his family was leaving the church. I was shocked! He didn't give specific details, but he explained that there had been a doctrinal disagreement between him and the group of elders. After several months of discussions and debates, the conflict could not be resolved.

I couldn't believe what I was hearing! Our parents, the spiritual leaders in the family of God, were going to be divorced!

How could this happen? I wondered with disbelief. *How can Christians argue? We have a big, powerful God! What could possibly be so bad that God couldn't handle it?*

Pastor Tom made it clear that he did not want the congregation to split, but it was inevitable. Several people stood and announced, "If Pastor Tom goes, my family will go with him."

How could I choose? Would I stay there or go with my pastor to start a new church?

Sunrise Ministries was housed in that church. *What would happen to my ministry? Why are they allowing this to happen?*

I didn't wait for answers, which was my first mistake. I dashed out of the church with a bomb ticking in my heart. I had to get away before it exploded.

Driving on the route to my home, tears blurred my vision. I turned into a parking lot and stopped my car.

The bomb exploded. I let the pain and confusion burst out of me.

Moments later, I rubbed my eyes, lifted my head and looked through the windshield. I was parked at the front door of a liquor store!

My raised eyebrows pulled my eyelids wide open. I felt like a policeman had stopped me and given me a very expensive speeding ticket, but I was innocent! I hadn't meant to be there!

Yet, here you are, a demon whispered. *How convenient!*

"No." I spoke in a low, trembling voice. I turned the key in the ignition.

Why not? You're so upset! A good, stiff drink is just what you need.

"No! I am not going to drink!" I backed out of the parking space and waited at the exit driveway for the traffic to clear.

Good girl. You should be proud of yourself. You cannot indulge in a mind-altering drug, like alcohol. If you would drink, you might cause a terrible wreck on the way home and kill someone! But a drag on a cigarette would calm you down.

I turned onto the street and floored the gas pedal, as if someone was chasing me.

A cigarette won't hurt anyone else. It might take a few years off of your life, when you're old, but you'll get to heaven that much sooner.

I saw a convenience store one block ahead.

Or, you could stop and get a candy bar.

I drove into the parking lot of the convenience store. There was a painful knot in my stomach, and I couldn't think of any food that sounded good.

A cigarette would be so good right now. Better than calories. You've gained so much weight since you quit smoking. It's embarrassing.

At this point, I wasn't sure if I was hearing my own thoughts or a demon's cunning craft.

"At least I got away from that liquor store," I congratulated myself. "A cigarette is the least of two evils," I mumbled and walked into the store.

The first one made me feel dizzy and drowsy, but I had finished the second cigarette by the time I got home. I sat on my couch smoking one cigarette after the other. I didn't change clothes and go to bed. I fell asleep on the couch, fully dressed, and there I had moped for two full days.

On Wednesday, Pastor Collins called again. Being a pastor, I was sure he would understand the heartache of a church split, so I explained, "We're a family. I love those people. All of them. Whether I stay at my church or go with Pastor Tom to start a new church, I will miss so many of my brothers and sisters! And, all of this is contrary to God's Word!" I heard bitterness rising in my voice. "This bickering is so trivial compared to the work God has called us to do!"

"Yes, it is," he agreed. "and one day soon, you will realize that your situation is so trivial compared to Jackie's."

I didn't reply. I knew he was right, but he didn't know the whole story, and I was too ashamed to tell him.

I didn't go to church that Wednesday night. I couldn't face, let alone deal with the absence of Pastor Tom. Instead, I mustered enough courage to phone Don and JoAnn Dehon, the founders of Sunrise Ministries, in Boulder, Colorado. I told them about the church split. They were empathetic, understanding the pain of broken relationships and the huge challenge of adjustments in the months ahead. Since they were feeling sorry enough for me, I mustered more courage to broach the real reason for my call. I told them I wanted to resign my position in Sunrise Ministries.

They wouldn't accept my resignation. They suggested taking a sabbatical for a month or two or whatever time I would need.

"There's more," I continued. "I bought a pack of cigarettes and started smoking again. I can't talk to people about their addictions to alcohol and other drugs, when I am addicted to nicotine."

"I do," Don replied.

The silence that followed was finally broken by the sound of Don's chuckling.

"I enjoy a pipe now and then. It's an addiction of sorts, because I have not thrown that pipe away. It's a thorn in my side, lust of my flesh. I'm not saying it's okay to smoke anything. I'm just saying that I'm not perfect, and you're not perfect, and God is not done working in our lives yet. He loves us enough to change us … in His perfect timing. In the meantime, He can still use us to help other people."

"But Christian leaders are supposed to be obedient. We're supposed to be striving to be 'perfect, as our Father in heaven is perfect.'" I was quoting a scripture with bitter sarcasm.

"Your perfectionism, my dear friend, is more of a problem for you than your smoking."

Tears filled my eyes. He had stabbed me, truthfully and lovingly, in a very tender spot. I promised to call him later, pulled the afghan over my head and fell asleep on the couch.

On Friday morning, Pastor Collins called again. "I have just one request," he said. "Will you pray for Jackie?"

He waited, while the sting of remorse pierced my heart. I hadn't even thought about praying for Jackie.

"Okay," I agreed. "I'll pray for Jackie." *But I don't know what good that will do,* I thought, *coming from me.*

I kept my promise. I prayed for Jackie every day for one week. They were short, obedient prayers, without compassion. I felt like I was talking to a brick wall.

Pastor Collins called at the end of that week. Very seriously, he said, "I am going to tell you something, and I hope you will understand the gravity of my persistence." He paused, then he spoke each word slowly, "God told me to call you."

A chill trickled through my body.

"When I heard that public service announcement on the radio, God spoke to me, and He told me to send Jackie to you."

I didn't want to believe him, but the shivering chill raised goose bumps all over my body, and I knew it was the hand of the Holy Spirit, squeezing my heart.

"Why didn't you mention this before?" I asked, dubiously.

"You must admit, you cut me off each time I called. When you told me about your pastor leaving, I thought I should give you some time … but time is running out for Jackie. She has not eaten anything all week. She won't open her mouth to eat or speak." He paused, then he spoke decidedly, "I will drive her to Wichita. We can be there in one hour."

"Okay," I whispered. "Bring her to my church. I'll be waiting outside in the playground area."

It was four o'clock when they arrived. Pastor Collins and I greeted each other as if we were old friends. He introduced me to Jackie.

She was so skinny! Sharp bones protruded at the collar of her blouse. Her cheek bones stuck out like hills next to black valleys beneath her eyes. She looked like a skeleton covered with a thin layer of skin.

I told Pastor Collins I would drive her back to his house that evening. He gave me his home address and phone number, then he drove away.

"Let's sit on the merry-go-round," I said cheerfully. I headed in that direction, then I turned to see if she was following. She had not moved from the place where Pastor Collins had left her. I walked back and put her hand in mine, gently pulling her. "Come on, Jackie."

As we walked the distance to the merry-go-round, hand in hand, I asked God to help me, praying silently from my heart. *I know I am not worthy, Lord, to speak for You ... but You can speak through me. Help me to tell Jackie exactly what You want her to know. And please, lift her out of this miry pit. In the name of Jesus.*

I sat next to Jackie on the merry-go-round and pushed the ground with my foot.

"I love merry-go-rounds," I said. "Makes me feel like a kid." I smiled as I talked. "I was older than you are when I first met Jesus. I was 32, going on 17." I laughed at myself. "From the time I started drinking, when I was 16, my emotional growth stopped, and I acted like a 16-year-old most of my adult life. But I'm glad I was like a kid, because that's the easiest way to get to know God. I believed what I read in the Bible, and miracles started happening in my life."

I told Jackie most of my testimony, starting with the night when I wanted to kill myself. Then being in the bright light, when God told me He loved me. "It didn't matter what I had done," I exclaimed. "God said He loved me when I was good, and He loved me when I was bad. He had loved me all of my life! What a relief that was! I had always thought I was unlovable."

After each story, I asked Jackie direct questions, but she didn't answer. It seemed she was ignoring me. I wondered if she could even hear what I was saying. Still, I kept pushing the ground slowly with my foot, and I kept telling her real-life testimonies.

I told Jackie the story about Robert trying to rape me. "I shouted, 'Get off me in the name of Jesus!' In a flash, Robert was flung clear across the bedroom. He slammed into that wall so hard, it knocked him out cold! That was enough for me to know there really is power in the name of Jesus!"

I described the huge, hairy spider and the lion that I had seen when I was going through withdrawal. "I prayed and surrendered my whole life to Jesus. Then He touched me and healed me, and I haven't had a drink since that day."

Two hours had passed. I had given a good performance, but it wasn't good enough to get Jackie to respond. It seemed nothing impressed her. The evening was almost dark. I was hungry, but what I really wanted was a cigarette, and I didn't think Jackie would care if I smoked.

I stood and stretched my arms. "I'd like to have a cigarette, but I shouldn't smoke on the church grounds. How would you like to go to a taco shop? It's not far. I can smoke there, and we'll have supper. My treat. Do you like tacos?"

Jackie lifted her head and looked at me. There was movement in her eyes as she studied my face curiously. "You mean … God loves you … even though you smoke?"

Oh, my gosh! She spoke! I felt the Holy Spirit stirring in me, like a gust of wind, and the force of it nearly knocked me over! *Answer her!*

"Yes! Of course God loves me! Even though I smoke."

She looked at the ground and kicked a rock with her foot. I watched her intently, holding my breath. When she looked up again, her eyes were full of tears.

"Do you think God could love me, too?" she asked.

I was stunned, knowing I was witnessing a miracle! After all of Pastor Collins' good efforts for three months, and after all of my good stories for two hours, God had ultimately used my weakness to show Jackie the depth of His love! The Holy Spirit's gentler nudge was like an elbow poking my ribs. *Answer her!*

"Yes, Jackie. Jesus loves you every bit as much as He loves me. Not more and not less."

"Really?" she asked with squinted eyes. "After everything I have done to my kids and my husband? Has Pastor Collins told you everything?"

"It doesn't matter what you've done. Jesus loves you just the way you are."

Jesus loves you just the way you are.

It seemed like an echo in my mind, but it wasn't my voice. It was the still, small voice of God, and He was speaking to me. Suddenly, I understood why God had told Pastor Collins to send Jackie to me. I needed to hear those very words.

Both of us were lifted out of miry pits that day. Jackie became one of my most dependable helpers and one of the most talkative witnesses, telling others about our wonderful Savior at the Sunrise Ministries support group meetings.

Chapter 11

In all things, give thanks

The year was 1994. I had a good job as production manager in the marketing department of a manufacturing company. I worked many overtime hours. November evenings were dark by 5:30 p.m.

One night, shortly after sunset, I became blurry-eyed, and I decided to quit working and go home much earlier than previously planned.

As I entered my driveway, I pushed the remote button to open my electric garage door, which made a loud noise. Before entering my garage, I noticed my large television console half in and half out of the front door of my house. Suspecting burglary in process, I went to a neighbor's house to call the police.

Two policemen inspected the interior shambles and reported that the burglars were gone. Before entering the house, I asked, "Is my dog alive?" When the policeman answered, "Yes," I began praising God.

Much damage had been done in my home and my VCR was gone, but my dog was fine and I was not harmed. I was grateful! Surely, God had made me sleepy, sending me home to interrupt the intruders.

For two hours, while the policemen wrote their reports and the photographer and fingerprint investigators did their work, I danced and laughed and gave thanks to God openly. The police team thought I was nuts.

"The VCR," I explained, "is just a thing that can be replaced."

One of the policemen, named Mark, asked, "Don't you feel violated?"

I happily replied, "To the contrary, I have been given a great opportunity! I will pray for the people who did this."

During the police team's investigation, I found a small seed, perhaps an apple seed, buried in broken glass on my bedroom floor. I was sure it was not mine. I deduced that the seed must have been dropped by the thieves. I glued the seed to my bedroom wall, beneath my wooden cross. "Every time I look at that seed," I told Mark, "I will pray for the robbers' salvation. God knows who they are, and someday I might meet them in heaven."

One hour after the police team had left, Mark came to my house and explained that a burglary had been reported nearby along with a description of the get-away car. Policemen had located and chased the car. Two men had gotten out of the car and had escaped on foot. They were not caught, but my VCR was found in the trunk of that car. Mark drove me to the scene of the confiscated car to identify my VCR.

Returning me home, Mark said, "This is a miracle! The odds of recovering an item on the same night it was stolen are one in a million! God must have done this for you, probably because you were not bitter or angry but actually thankful!"

My reply jolted him. "No. I don't think God did this for me. He knows I don't care about that VCR. More likely, everything that has happened tonight was for your benefit. God wanted you to see and hear and feel the joy of knowing Jesus."

Mark met Jesus that night, sitting in his police car in my driveway, and he asked Jesus to be his Lord and Savior.

Being thankful and joyful, even though my home had been invaded and vandalized, may not seem normal … but it is in the Kingdom of God. It's the best way to live!

Chapter 12

My white picket fence

I had my first alcoholic drink at age 16. I was a daily, addicted drinker for 16 years until the age of 32 when Jesus Christ saved me and delivered me from alcoholism. I walked with the Lord and talked with Him and grew in spiritual maturity over the next 13 years.

I was still single at age 45. I asked the Lord if he had a husband in mind for me, and my thoughts about that grew from leery to curious to excited. Many of my friends and relatives thought I would never get married because I was too picky. Perhaps because I was, indeed. I'd made a list of 27 attributes that I would like to have in a husband, and I gave it to the Lord.

My good friend, Janice Harvey, lived in Hilo, Hawaii. She had a good friend, Joan Flores, who lived in Irving, Texas. I knew of Janice-and-Joan's friendship, but I had never met Joan. It was during Joan's visit at Janice's home that she saw a photograph of me and asked about me.

Janice explained that I had moved from Wichita, Kansas to Shell Knob, Missouri, on Table Rock Lake five months earlier. I had finally secured a good job (a rarity in this rural area) as Advertising Manager for three small-town newspapers and was determined to fulfill a life-long dream of living on this lake, which had been my family's summer haven since 1971. I loved all of the lake activities. Most of all, fishing.

That sparked interest in Joan because she had a very good friend in Irving who was an avid fisherman, and he had just bought a brand new Champion bass boat. Joan returned to Texas and prompted Mike to call me. After five years of singleness, Mike had accepted single life. He enjoyed his job as a Flight Attendant with American Airlines. He was happy enough, and phoning me required a bit of prodding from Joan. She persisted because the nudge she felt from the Holy Spirit was real.

Mike and I enjoyed interesting, comfortable, long and frequent phone conversations for five months. We shared facts and figures, thoughts and opinions, experiences, hopes and dreams, but the most enticing aspect of our phone friendship was that we laughed a lot, easily and heartily. Although we had not yet met face-to-face, he sent a huge array of 12 red roses on Valentine's Day. That inspired a poem that I wrote that evening. The title was *Long Distance Romance,* and the next day I mailed the poem to Mike. It was inviting enough to lure him to Missouri.

Long Distance Romance

By Jo Dinsmoor

Meeting on the phone was safe and easy.
Make-up, manicure and fresh breath didn't matter.
The sound of your voice had thick dark hair
with a sprinkling of salt, and I liked your laugh.
Your photo arrived and, though your hair was barely there,
I still liked your laugh.

The miles between us were the locked bathroom door,
and each conversation as warm and relaxing
as a bubble bath at the end of a frazzled day.

Weeks told of hobbies, goals and opinions,
but months undressed your soul.
The card attached to the roses
exposed that four-letter word.
The time has come to see and touch,
to smell and taste what I've heard.

Intrigue is like the kindling of a fire.
Small, thin branches already aflame,
offering hope of a long-lasting blaze.
Watching and waiting for a spark to lure
heavy logs into giving their lives
for the warmth and light of the flame.

Suspense is in the cold, hard bark of the logs.
They're wise and cautious,
having stood so many years in the forest,
watching lovers come and go.
The logs lay on a bed of ashes
that once was alive with passion,
now dead and grey, easily blown away
with a whisper of good-bye.
But the logs are strong
with thick layers of character and courage.
Their roots had been deep.
They were nourished and prepared
for this purpose.

Love is the flame that finally
grows tall without flickering.
It leaps from log to log,
spreading itself to those who are willing
to make the commitment,
accepting each log just as it is,
regardless of where it has been before.
They become one,
with all the power and might to destroy,
or to glow and brighten a dark room.
It's very hot, raging throughout the longest night.
If it's a good fire, it will still be warm in the morning,
shimmering red beneath a blanket of soft, white ash,
exhausted but gratified that it lived and died for love.

Let's meet before the roses wilt.
I'll clean the house and do my nails
and bring the firewood in.

We met face-to-face on March 14, 1997, and we got married six weeks later. The instant we saw each other we knew we were meant to be together. My dog, Lady, was very protective, and she did not like men. She always growled at men; but when Mike walked into my house the first time, Lady sat close to him and laid her head on his lap. If I hadn't already been well aware of God's leading, I would have been shocked. There were other interesting signs of approval that might sound silly but were meaningful to me. I was totally satisfied that Mike had 24 of the 27 qualities on my list.

In April, two weeks before we were married, I met Mike's parents and several relatives at a family gathering in Farmington, Missouri. One week before we were married, Mike met my mother, my older sister and several friends at a reception in Wichita, Kansas. A few days before our wedding, we were counseled by the minister who conducted our wedding. It was quick but proper and blessed by God.

Before I married Mike, I asked him to read this book so that he would know everything about my past and, more importantly, the miraculous transformations God had made in me.

In August of that summer, I had to go to Wichita to help my mother for a weekend. When I returned and drove into our driveway, what I saw filled my heart with amazement and my eyes with tears. Mike had built a white picket fence, so "everyone who drove by our home would see it and know that the woman living there was normal."